T0311988

"This initial book in an exciting new series looks at one of the key global issues with which religion is intimately involved: the sustainable development goals. This punchy, thoughtful and comprehensive overview of the relevant issues is a must-read for scholars, practitioners and university students. It will help set the focus of debates on this issue. I warmly recommend it".

Jeffrey Haynes, London Metropolitan University, UK

"The 'Religion Matters' series is a timely and accessible compendium contextualizing the role of religion within the critical issues of our time. The first volume, *On the Significance of Religion in Conflict and Conflict Resolution*, demonstrates through careful analysis and illustrative case studies around the three Abrahamic traditions the real yet complex impact of religion in the global sphere, showing clearly the need for collaboration and understanding across sectors and religious traditions in conflict resolution. Building upon the rich academic expertise and lived experiences of the authors, and situating itself within the broader religion and peacebuilding scholarship of recent decades, this volume raises to the forefront the 'how' and 'why' religion does indeed matter".

Melissa Nozell, United States Institute of Peace, USA

"'Does religion matter' is a crucial question for billions of people around the world. Although in recent years, many governments and international organizations have begun considering the role of religion in policy, nevertheless these efforts remain in their initial phase. This edited volume creatively tackles this central issue in international politics. Combining several real and challenging cases, the Editors successfully dispel the myth that religion alone causes violent conflicts and is responsible for their solutions. The book also illustrates how the three Abrahamic traditions can be deployed effectively to positively contribute to conflict resolution and peacebuilding in Israeli Palestinian, Pakistan, and Rwanda settings. The edited volume adds an important voice to the field of interreligious peacebuilding. It also responds to the need for further engagement between policy makers and peacebuilding communities and practitioners".

Mohammed Abu-Nimer, American University School, USA

"This volume is an important contribution to efforts to bring religion back into the mainstream of conflict resolution and peacebuilding. Analyzing religion's role in conflict and peace by applying a simple framework to several rich case studies, the authors convincingly demonstrate that religion matters for anyone working in the field of conflict resolution today".

Owen Frazer, Center for Security Studies, Zurich, Switzerland

ON THE SIGNIFICANCE OF RELIGION IN CONFLICT AND CONFLICT RESOLUTION

In this ground-breaking volume, the authors analyze the role of religion in conflict and conflict resolution. They do so from the perspectives of Judaism, Christianity, and Islam, while bringing different disciplines into play, including peace and conflict studies, religious studies, theology, and ethics. With much of current academic, political, and public attention focusing on the conflictive dimensions of religion, this book also explores the constructive resources of religion for conflict resolution and reconciliation.

Analyzing the specific contributions of religious actors in this field, their potentials, and possible problems connected with them, this book sheds light on the concrete contours of the oftentimes vague "religious factor" in processes of social change. Case studies in current and former settings of violent conflict such as Israel, post-genocide Rwanda, and Pakistan provide "real-life" contexts for discussion.

Combining cutting-edge research with case studies and concrete implications for academics, policy makers, and practitioners, this concise and easily accessible volume helps to build bridges between these oftentimes separated spheres of engagement.

Christine Schliesser is a Senior Lecturer in Systematic Theology and Ethics at Zurich University, Switzerland, and a Research Fellow at Stellenbosch University, South Africa.

S. Ayse Kadayifci-Orellana is a Research Affiliate at Georgetown Institute for Women, Peace and Security at Georgetown University and a Senior Fellow at the Center for Global Policy, USA.

Pauline Kollontai is Professor of Higher Education in Theology and Religious Studies at York St John University, UK.

RELIGION MATTERS: ON THE SIGNIFICANCE OF RELIGION IN GLOBAL ISSUES

Edited by Christine Schliesser, Zurich University, Switzerland, S. Ayse Kadayifci-Orellana, Georgetown University, US, and Pauline Kollontai, York St John University, UK.

Policy makers, academics and practitioners worldwide are increasingly paying attention to the role of religion in global issues. This development is clearly noticeable in conflict resolution, development or climate change, to name just a few pressing issues of global relevance. Up to now, no book series has yet attempted to analyze the role of religion in current global issues in a coherent and systematic way that pertains to academics, policy makers and practitioners alike. The Sustainable Development Goals (SDGs) serve as a dynamic frame of reference. "Religion Matters" provides cutting-edge scholarship in a concise format and accessible language, thereby addressing academics, practitioners and policy makers.

ON THE SIGNIFICANCE OF RELIGION IN CONFLICT AND CONFLICT RESOLUTION
CHRISTINE SCHLIESSER, S. AYSE KADAYIFCI-ORELLANA AND PAULINE KOLLONTAI

For more information about this series, please visit:
https://www.routledge.com/religion/series/RELMAT

ON THE SIGNIFICANCE OF RELIGION IN CONFLICT AND CONFLICT RESOLUTION

Christine Schliesser
S. Ayse Kadayifci-Orellana
Pauline Kollontai

LONDON AND NEW YORK

First published 2021
by Routledge
2 Park Square, Milton Park, Abingdon, Oxon OX14 4RN

and by Routledge
52 Vanderbilt Avenue, New York, NY 10017

Routledge is an imprint of the Taylor & Francis Group, an informa business

British Library Cataloguing-in-Publication Data
A catalogue record for this book is available from the British Library

Library of Congress Cataloging-in-Publication Data
Names: Schliesser, Christine, 1977– author. | Kadayifci, Ayse S., author. |
Kollontai, Pauline, author.
Title: On the significance of religion in conflict and conflict resolution /
Christine Schliesser, S. Ayse Kadayifci-Orellana, Pauline Kollontai.
Description: Abingdon, Oxon; New York, NY: Routledge, 2020. |
Series: Religion matters: on the significance of religion in global issues |
Includes bibliographical references and index.
Identifiers: LCCN 2020006982 | ISBN 9780367459611 (hardback) |
ISBN 9780367433925 (paperback) | ISBN 9781003002888 (ebook)
Subjects: LCSH: Peace–Religious aspects. |
Conflict management–Religious aspects.
Classification: LCC BL65.P4 S385 2020 | DDC 201/.76332–dc23
LC record available at https://lccn.loc.gov/2020006982

ISBN: 978-0-367-45961-1 (hbk)
ISBN: 978-0-367-43392-5 (pbk)
ISBN: 978-1-003-00288-8 (ebk)

Typeset in Bembo
by Newgen Publishing UK

CONTENTS

NOTES ON THE AUTHORS

Christine Schliesser is a Senior Lecturer for Systematic Theology and Ethics at Zurich University, Switzerland. She is also a Research Fellow in Studies in Historical Trauma and Transformation at Stellenbosch University, South Africa. Coming from the perspective of Christian theology and ethics, she has a sustained interest in the role of theology and religion(s) in public life. In particular, Christine Schliesser explores the role of religious actors in national reconciliation processes after historical trauma such as in Rwanda and South Africa. Next to peace and reconciliation studies, she focuses in her work on the theology and ethics of Dietrich Bonhoeffer, public theology, and the role of religion in sustainable development. Her recent publications include *Alternative Approaches in Conflict Resolution* (eds. Christine Schliesser and Martin Leiner, Palgrave Macmillan 2018) and *Theologie im öffentlichen Ethikdiskurs* (EVA Leipzig 2019).

S. Ayse Kadayifci-Orellana is currently a Research Affiliate at Georgetown Institute for Women, Peace and Security at Georgetown University, a Senior Fellow at the Center for Global Peace, and Adjunct Professor at Georgetown University MA Program in Conflict Resolution, where she also served as the Assistant Professor and Associate Director. Prior to that, she worked as a consultant for the Religion and Peacebuilding Program at the United States Institute of Peace, and as an Assistant Professor at the School of International Service at American University, Washington DC, before commencing at Georgetown University. She is also one of the founding members, where she served as the Associate Director at the Salam Institute for Peace and Justice (2005–2012). S. Ayse Kadayifci-Orellana has also authored *Standing on an Isthmus: Islamic Narratives of War and Peace in the Palestinian Territories* (Lexington Books 2007), and co-authored *Islam and Peace and Conflict Resolution in Islam: Precept and Practice* (University Press of America 2001).

Pauline Kollontai is Professor of Higher Education in Theology and Religious Studies at York St John University (YSJU) and is the Director for the Centre for Religion in Society. She was appointed as a member of the Resident Research Inter-disciplinary Seminar Programme Team on "Religion and Violence" from January–May 2019 at the Centre of Theological Inquiry, Princeton. Previously she worked at the University of Leeds in the School of Adult Education and at the University of Bradford in the Department of Peace Studies. Her academic qualifications are in the disciplines of Peace Studies and Theology, and Religious Studies. She combines these disciplines in her research focusing on religion, peace, violence, and reconciliation in various global contexts. This includes examining the role of faith-based actors, gender and peacebuilding, as well as religion, democracy, and rights. Pauline Kollontai is the author of several peer-reviewed articles and chapters and her recent edited books include *Mediating Peace: Reconciliation through Visual Art, Music and Film* (Cambridge Scholars Press 2015) and *The Role of Religion in Peacebuilding: Crossing the Boundaries of Prejudice and Distrust* (Jessica Kingsley Publishers 2017).

FOREWORD

Religion Matters. All three of us share this common conviction, even though we come from different religious traditions, disciplinary backgrounds, and geographical contexts. Religion matters, not only in private and personal lives, but also in the public sphere. This means that religion also matters when it comes to addressing today's challenges, including conflict and conflict resolution, economic inequality, migration and climate change, to mention a few. While the role of religion in these contexts is being increasingly acknowledged by academics, policy makers, and practitioners, the "religious factor" often remains vague. How exactly does religion matter? What role do religious actors actually play? What are their specific potentials and problems?

It is the goal of this book series, titled "Religion Matters: On the Significance of Religion in Global Issues", of which this book, *On the Significance of Religion in Conflict and Conflict Resolution* is the first volume to address precisely these questions. We realize that the complexity of today's challenges—as expressed in the 17 Sustainable Development Goals (SDGs)—requires the joint effort of different religious and disciplinary voices, and the cooperation of all relevant actors, including academics, policy makers, and practitioners. This series thus seeks to build bridges—between disciplines, religious traditions, and actors. For it is in the joint effort of all that the potentials for change are phenomenal.

As this volume shows, today's greatest challenges include conflict and conflict resolution. SDG 16 thus expresses the need for "peace, justice and strong institutions". If acknowledged at all, religion is oftentimes perceived in conflicts as part of the problem rather than as part of the solution. In this first volume of "Religion Matters" we examine not only the conflictive sides of religion, but also its potentials for overcoming violence and for reconciliation. Three different case studies from the perspectives of three different religions—Judaism, Christianity, and Islam—demonstrate how religious traditions have been used to both increase conflict and foster conflict resolution.

The idea for this volume, and series, evolved from an interdisciplinary, interreligious, and international resident research seminar convened by the Center for Theological Inquiry (CTI) in Princeton on "Religion and Violence" in 2019 and led by CTI director Dr. William Storrar and associate director Dr. Joshua Mauldin. To that end, we wish to express our gratitude to everyone who played a part in making this volume a reality. We particularly want to thank the members of our research group for their encouragement, comments, and critique. We also extend our thanks to our international, interreligious, and interdisciplinary Series Advisory Board for their support. We are privileged to have found with Regina Baumann a visual artist, who not only shares our vision and commitment through her artwork but also inspires us through her powerful cover images. Thank you, Regina.

One of the goals of this series is to be as easily accessible as possible, which today means Open Access. We therefore would like to thank the Institute for Social Ethics (Zurich University), the Faculty of Theology (Zurich University), and Centre for Religion in Society (York St John University) for their financial support of the Open Access version of this volume. A further thanks is extended to Dr. Lee-Anne Roux for her wonderful support with the editorial process. We also express our sincere thanks to Routledge, namely Rebecca Shillabeer and Dr. Amy Doffegnies, for their excellent collaboration.

Zurich, Washington, DC, and York, November 2019
Christine Schliesser
S. Ayse Kadayifci-Orellana
Pauline Kollontai

ACKNOWLEDGMENTS

Title of the cover photo of Regina Baumhauer's work:
"Open Letter, Focus" 2005; Materials used: Oil, graphite and acrylics on canvas;
120 cm x 120 cm/48" x 48"
Religion matters / learning from the past / acknowledging the world as global / embracing the future
Focus with our eyes / and minds / and with our hearts / to see and understand the problems
Focus with our eyes / and minds / and with our hearts / to work for the Sustainable Development Goals for a better world / SDG 16 and SDG 17
Regina Baumhauer
New York, November 9, 2019
https://rbaumhauer.wixsite.com/reginabaumhauer

ABBREVIATIONS

ADEPR	Pentecostal Church of Rwanda
AIDS	acquired immune deficiency syndrome
BDHRL	Bureau of Democracy, Human Rights, and Labor
CARSA	Christian Action for Reconciliation and Social Assistance
CIA	Central Intelligence Agency
CSS	Center for Security Studies
FATA	Federally Administered Tribal Areas
FBO	faith-based organization
HDI	Human Development Index
HIV	human immunodeficiency virus
ICAN	International Civil Society Action Network
ICG	International Crisis Group
ICRC	International Committee of the Red Cross
ICRD	International Center for Religion and Diplomacy
IDF	Israeli Defense Force
IJR	Institute for Justice and Reconciliation
IMFA	Israeli Ministry of Foreign Affairs
IRCSL	Inter-Religious Council of Sierra Leone
ISIS	Islamic State of Iraq and Syria
JeM	Jaish-e-Mohammed
JI	Jamaat-e-Islami

JNF	Jewish National Fund
JUI	Jamiat-e Ulama Islam
KP	Khyber Pakhtunkhwa
LeT	Lashkar-e-Taiba
NGO	non-governmental organization
NIV	New International Version
NURC	National Unity and Reconciliation Commission
NUSAF	Northern Uganda Social Action Fund
OECD	Organisation for Economic Co-operation and Development
PAG	Pentecostal Assembly of God
PAIMAN	PAIMAN Alumni Trust
PEC	Peacebuilding Evaluation Consortium
PLO	Palestinian Liberation Organization
PTSD	post-traumatic stress disorder
RHR	Rabbis for Human Rights
RPF	Rwanda Patriotic Front
RUF	Revolutionary United Front
SDGs	Sustainable Development Goals
SFP	School of Peace
SNSF	Swiss National Science Foundation
TTP	Tehrik-i-Taliban
UEM	United Evangelical Mission
UN	United Nations
UNCCP	United Nations Conciliation Commission for Palestine
UNESCO	United Nations Educational, Scientific and Cultural Organization
UNHCR	United Nations High Commissioner for Refugees
UNIATF	United Nations Interagency Task Force
UN OCHA	United Nations Office for the Coordination of Humanitarian Affairs
US	United States
USAID	United States Agency for International Development
WASNS	Wahat al-Salam – Neve Shalom
WPS	Women, Peace, and Security
YSJU	York St John University

PART I
SUMMARY

1

SUMMARY AND IMPLICATIONS FOR ACADEMICS, POLICY MAKERS, AND PRACTITIONERS

Christine Schliesser, S. Ayse Kadayifci-Orellana, and Pauline Kollontai

Religion matters in conflict and conflict resolution. Effective conflict resolution is too complex an endeavor to forego the contributions of any relevant actor, religious or not. It is therefore vital to better understand the role of religion in conflict and to strengthen religion's positive contributions for conflict resolution. It is in the joint collaboration of academics, policy makers, and practitioners, religious and secular, that the potential for change is astounding.

IMPLICATION 1: BRIDGING THE DIVIDE BETWEEN RELIGIOUS AND SECULAR

Effective conflict resolution depends on both religious and secular actors. Each must overcome ignorance and prejudices in order to collaborate successfully. For secular actors in government, business, media, and higher education, this calls for strengthening religious literacy. For religious actors, this means endorsing a theology that promotes the public and collaborative sides of religion.

IMPLICATION 2: BRIDGING THE DIVIDE BETWEEN DIFFERENT FAITH TRADITIONS

Besides the necessity for bridging the religious–secular divide, there is a need for more and deeper cooperation between different faith traditions in conflict resolution. More often than not, ignorance and prejudices hinder interfaith cooperation. Interfaith dialogue and joint initiatives, however, can serve as powerful inspirations for overcoming violence not only within a particular conflict but also far beyond it.

IMPLICATION 3: BRIDGING THE DIVIDE BETWEEN ACADEMICS, POLICY MAKERS, AND PRACTITIONERS

Effective conflict resolution depends on the collaborative efforts of all relevant actors—academics, policy makers, and practitioners. Joint and cross-over efforts in higher education, governments, non-governmental organizations (NGOs), and faith-based organizations (FBOs) need to be supported.

IMPLICATION 4: MORE EVALUATION

Despite the increasing number of programs focusing on religious peacebuilding, there is a knowledge gap in the area of evaluation. Evaluation of religious peacebuilding generates better understanding of what is effective religious peacebuilding and supports evidence-based policy and practice.

IMPLICATION 5: BETTER INCLUSION OF WOMEN

Women are often marginalized in conflict resolution processes, and consequently their perspectives and experiences are excluded. Recent studies show, however, that women are particularly effective agents of social change and conflict resolution.

IMPLICATION 6: BETTER INCLUSION OF THE YOUTH

At the same time, more attention in conflict resolution theory and praxis must be directed towards the youth. The so-called "youth bulge" in many countries of the Global South has already given rise to concern about the potential destabilizing effect. The same goes for concerns about the growth of destablizing and anti-democratic ideologies such as racism, white supremacy, and Islamophobia amongst youth in the Global North. At the same time, the tremendous potential for conflict resolution and reconciliation within children and youth goes largely neglected.

IMPLICATION 7: BETTER ENGAGEMENT OF THE MEDIA

Conflict resolution in general, and religious conflict resolution in particular, need to become better in strategically engaging the media and social media. While there is no shortage of media outlets preaching religious hatred and intolerance, religious peacebuilders have to catch up in employing these powerful instruments for the means of peace, empathy, and acceptance of the other.

IMPLICATION 8: TAKING THE ISSUES OF PROSELYTIZATION AND INSTRUMENTALIZATION INTO ACCOUNT

Religious actors often face the charge that their main goal is to attract followers and convert others, which can constitute a serious impediment to peacebuilding between religious groups. At the same time, one needs to acknowledge that conversion is not an exclusively religious phenomenon as all development organizations aim to transform the way people act and think in terms of citizenship for the common good. This sensitive subject should therefore be treated in a differentiated manner and framed under the aspects of transparency and equality.

IMPLICATION 9: BETTER ENGAGEMENT OF INDIGENOUS AND NON-ABRAHAMIC RELIGIONS

With much of Western attention focusing on the Abrahamic religions—Judaism, Christianity, and Islam—in conflict resolution, little attention is being paid to the contributions of indigenous, dharmic, and other East Asian religious traditions. Similar to Abrahamic faiths, these traditions have a wealth of resources and values that promote peacebuilding and justice.

PART II
WHY RELIGION MATTERS

2

WHY RELIGION MATTERS
AN INTRODUCTION

Christine Schliesser, S. Ayse Kadayifci-Orellana, and Pauline Kollontai

At a conference on poverty alleviation a couple of years ago in Salzburg, Austria, I (Christine Schliesser) presented a paper on the religious factor in development. During the Q&A session, a renowned economist from Frankfurt, Germany, stood up, saying: "I am surprised that you would bring religion into this context. We all know that religion is a private affair and has no bearing on public issues such as development". "I am surprised that you are surprised", I replied, "Because we all should know that religion matters in global affairs". Religion matters, indeed. Not only does it affect the everyday choices, behavior, and action of countless people worldwide, but religion also has an impact on global issues and challenges, including conflict and conflict resolution, development, and climate change.

THE QUESTION IS NOT IF, BUT HOW RELIGION MATTERS. OR: THE FAILURE OF THE SECULARIZATION THESIS

Much of public and academic discourse in the past decades was dominated by the so-called "secularization thesis", claiming that modern societies would become more and more secular, while religion was retreating. The secularization thesis was reinforced by the post-Enlightenment proposition that religion belongs to the private sphere, while all matters of public, let alone global concern, ought to be treated as purely secular (and this conviction is still very much alive, as the economist from Frankfurt cited above demonstrates). Recent years, however, have seen signs of an impending paradigm change. Instead of a "disenchantment of the world" (Max Weber), we find a renewed interest in the role of religion in the making of modern societies. A "return to the question of religion" (Freeman 2012: 1), even a "desecularization of the world" (ed. Berger 1999), is now being proclaimed. Along with the failure of the secularization thesis to explain the resurgence of religion in many societal and political processes worldwide, this thesis is further contested by recent empirical findings. According to a 2015 study conducted by the Pew Research Center, the 21st century will be a religious one. All main religions—except for Buddhism—will experience growth in numbers. By 2050, the number of Muslims will have increased to equal Christianity and 10 percent of Europeans will adhere to Islam (Pew Research Center 2015).

The increasing awareness of the significance of religion on global issues has become apparent not only in academics, but also amongst practitioners and policy makers. Paradigmatic for this is the 2016 European Union's appointment of the first ever Special Envoy for the promotion of freedom of religion or belief outside the European Union. This appointment stands for the recognition of the link between the right of freedom of religion, conscience, and thought, on the one hand, and public issues such as stability and peace on the other hand. As the Council of the European Union states: "Violations of freedom of religion or belief may exacerbate intolerance and often constitute early indicators of potential violence and conflicts" (Council of the European Union 2013: 1).

The question is therefore no longer *if* religion makes a contribution in processes of social change, but rather *of what kind* are these contributions and what are their specific potentials and problems. In order to better understand the impact of religion on different issues of public concern, various national governments in secularized, Western countries have started to establish special units. The United States, for example, created the "Office of Religion and Global Affairs" at the State Department, while the UK set up the CONSENT strategy at the Home Office, with an emphasis on understanding the role of religion in promoting radicalization and terrorism, and Switzerland's Federal Department of Foreign Affairs' Human Security Division formed a task force on "Religion, politics and conflicts".

BRINGING TOGETHER ACADEMICS, POLICY MAKERS, AND PRACTITIONERS

With academics, policy makers, and practitioners becoming increasingly aware of the importance of understanding the religious factor in public and global affairs, it would seem only natural that all of these relevant actors join forces. Yet ignorance and suspicion on all sides remain high, further perpetuated by the divides between religious and non-religious actors and between actors of different faith traditions. This observation is part of the rationale behind this book and the entire book series. In view of the complexity and urgency of the challenges presented to us as global citizens, we simply cannot afford to ignore the wisdom, insights, and experiences by any one actor. Coming together from the Jewish, Christian, and Muslim faith traditions, we want to connect the contributions of our respective religions and our respective disciplines. It is our aim and hope that this book series will help to build bridges across different faith traditions, different disciplines, and between academics, policy makers, and practitioners. We are encouraged to see more and more of these cross-boundaries initiatives emerge. One example is the 2016 conference "Partners for Change. Religions and the 2030 Agenda for Sustainable Development". This high-profile conference was initiated by the German Federal Ministry for Economic Cooperation and Development and brought together actors from politics, religion, and NGOs to jointly explore the role of religion in pressing issues such as peace, poverty, and climate change.

SITUATING OUR WORK: THE SUSTAINABLE DEVELOPMENT GOALS

To our great fortune, we thus do not need to invent a framework that situates our work. It is already present in that grand global task spelled out to each one of us in the 17 Sustainable Development

Goals (SDGs). These goals, adopted by all United Nations member states in 2015, include many of the world community's most pressing challenges, such as ending poverty and hunger, reducing inequality, and working for peace and justice. In achieving these goals, the SDGs call for a global partnership between both developed and developing countries, between the so-called Global North and the Global South. The SDGs further recognize the intrinsic relationship between the individual goals. Ending hunger, for instance, is linked to ending violent conflicts, currently the number one driving force of hunger. At the same time, efforts at reducing inequality will only be sustainable if they are connected to tackling climate change and efforts to preserve our forests and oceans. Describing this bigger picture, UN Secretary General António Guterres states: "We need a global response that addresses the root causes of conflict, and integrates peace, sustainable development and human rights in a holistic way – from conception to execution" (Guterres 2017). So while the different volumes of the series "Religion Matters" all address specific global issues—related directly or indirectly to the SDGs—we always need to remind ourselves that these issues are connected with one another and cannot be treated in isolation. This volume with its focus on conflict and conflict resolution relates most directly to SDG 16 ("Peace, Justice and Strong Institutions"), yet connects to a number of other SDGs such as SDG 1 ("No Poverty"), SDG 2 ("Zero Hunger"), SDG 3 ("Good Health and Well-Being"), SDG 4 ("Quality Education"), and SDG 17 ("Partnerships for the Goals"). Having said that, we need to turn to the task of finding a common language. This entails a working definition of what we mean by "religion" and by "conflict resolution".

WHAT ARE WE TALKING ABOUT? DEFINING OUR TERMS

Religion. Religion is notoriously hard to define and is usually framed in terms of substantial (referring to some kind of content or dogma) vs. functional (referring to the function of religion, such as creating identities or in- and outsiders) definitions. We have found it most helpful to work with a pragmatic understanding of religion. This means that we understand religion simply as what is described and understood as religion by our interlocutors and the communities we work with (Waardenburg 1986). We understand religion, furthermore, as inherently ambivalent. While it can be used to ignite and support strife and violence, it also contains potent resources for overcoming violence and for promoting reconciliation. With much of public and academic attention focused on the conflictive sides of religion, we also explore its constructive features.

In order to better operationalize the structural dimensions of collective religious actors, we work with the term FBO. With Julia Berger (2003: 1) we define FBOs as

> formal organizations whose identity and mission are self-consciously derived from the teachings of one or more religious or spiritual traditions and which operate on a non-profit, independent, voluntary basis to promote and realize collectively articulated ideas about the public good at the national or international level.

Conflict Resolution. Conflict in and of itself is ethically neutral. It can be constructive, leading to fruitful individual and social change, yet it can also result in destructiveness and violence. It is the latter that we are concerned with here. The field of conflict resolution as a subject matter for academics, policy makers, and practitioners is continuously evolving (Kriesberg 2009). Up until now, we cannot boast of a single overarching theory or agreement on scope, approaches, and methods. Rather than as a distinct approach or a separate discipline, conflict resolution is best described as a mode of constructively dealing with conflict that aims for solutions beneficial to all sides involved, while minimizing the use of violence. It is interdisciplinary, makes use of a variety of approaches and engages both theory and practice. Other terms often encountered in this field include conflict transformation, peacebuilding, peacemaking, and reconciliation, with each having a different focus. Our understanding of conflict resolution is inclusive of all these concepts. By paying attention to different dimensions of violence—personal, structural, and cultural (Galtung 1969)—conflict resolution deals with preventing conflicts, stopping acute violence and post-conflict work.

DESCRIPTIVE OR NORMATIVE? UNIVERSAL OR PARTICULAR? ON BECOMING TRANSPARENT

We believe that any helpful approach to understanding the role of religion in global issues, such as conflict and conflict resolution, benefits from listening to the insights of state-of-the-art scholarship in these fields. Yet these theoretical insights need to be supplemented by practical examples of how these approaches, methods, or models play out in real-life contexts, or conversely, don't play out. This is why we include case studies. Our case studies on Israel, Rwanda, and Pakistan were chosen to provide examples of the role of religion in different cultural and religious contexts. They are conducted from our own specific points of view that we lay out below. This includes our own academic discipline, our cultural background, our experiences as on the ground, and the faith tradition we associate ourselves with. We don't believe in the possibility of absolute neutrality and objectivity—another example of post-Enlightenment propositions that the academic world has accepted for too long without questioning. Each scholar, each policy maker, and each practitioner is shaped in his and her perspectives by a variety of factors, including one's professional background, personal upbringing, and perception of reality. Instead of pretending that genuinely neutral, value-free judgments are possible (or even desirable), we rather argue for the need to make one's own particular perspective transparent.

Rejecting the possibility of a truly objective position does not mean rejecting the possibility of (self-)criticism. On the contrary, immanent criticism is very much part of the particular perspective. So while we acknowledge our own particular tradition—for instance, as a female, white, Jewish, Western academic-practitioner—we do engage in active self-criticism of this very tradition. Are, then, our case studies done from a descriptive or normative framework? We combine both. While we seek to provide the most accurate description possible of a certain context, such as through ethnographic methods, we also include normative claims. For instance, if certain theological concepts in pre-genocide Rwanda were abused to build tensions between the different ethnicities, these problematical hermeneutics will be criticized from within the Christian-theological tradition. Normative reasoning thus supplements descriptive accounts.

OUTLINE OF THIS BOOK

The outline of this book mirrors its approach in that it is interreligious, interdisciplinary, and international, with the explicit aim to be relevant to academics, policy makers, and practitioners. Preceded by an executive summary (Part I) and this introduction (Part II), the analytical heart of the book consists of two main parts (Parts III and IV), discussing both the conflictive sides of religion and its resources of overcoming conflict. After providing a general orientation into each field, we utilize three case studies to explore how this is spelled out in concrete conflict situations. Each case study discusses the role of one particular faith tradition in a certain conflict, critically analyzed by a representative of that religion. Through using the same case studies in Part III and Part IV, we emphasize the inescapable ambivalence of religion in containing both conflictive and constructive resources often at work in one and the same context (Appleby 2000). The final part (Part V) draws together the insights gained from the case studies and spells out concrete implications for academics, policy makers, and practitioners.

PART III: RELIGION MATTERS IN CONFLICT

ORIENTATION

Part III focuses on the conflictive dimension of religion and asks: Did religion do it? We discuss some of the most relevant models available for helping us to understand this role. We find the work of Owen Frazer, Richard Friedli, and Mark Owen particularly helpful (Frazer and Owen 2018; Frazer and Friedli 2015). By combining their approaches, we discuss six ways of thinking about religion, namely: religion as community, as a set of teachings, as spirituality, as practice, as discourse, and as institution. The work of Robert Eisen, like that of R. Scott Appleby, focuses on how the interpretation of religious foundational texts can inspire adherents to engage in either peace or conflict, and points out that the reading of these texts are also dependent on external factors in the political, economic and social spheres (Eisen 2011). This orientation will be followed by three case studies, spelling out the concrete implications of religion in different conflicts.

JEWISH PERSPECTIVE: RELIGION IN ISRAEL'S LAND RIGHTS CONFLICTS

Kollontai's perspective is from the standpoint of religious studies. Using a Jewish lens, she discusses how Judaism in Israel, which is both a democratic and Jewish state, contributes to the state's continuing ideological struggle over land rights within Israel. Three issues are explored: (1) the nature of the relationship between Judaism and the state, (2) a theology of the land which abandons care for the stranger/neighbor, and (3) the Jewish establishment's discourse promoting and supporting state policy of further Judaization of land in Southern Israel. In presenting these issues, Kollontai will concentrate on the growth of hard-line political views amongst Israel's political leaders, accompanied by increasing influence of the Orthodox/Ultra-Orthodox Jewish establishments on government through political appointments and presence of their political parties in the Knesset. Opposition is being reinforced against a land for peace compromise whether with the Palestinians or Israel's Arab citizens.

CHRISTIAN PERSPECTIVE: RELIGION IN PRE-GENOCIDE AND GENOCIDE RWANDA

Schliesser, coming from the perspective of Christian theology and ethics, traces the role of religion in helping to create and sustain an environment in which the Rwandan genocide could occur in 1994 in which up to one million children, women, and men were killed. She identifies four factors, including the (too) close relationship between Church and state, the churches' support of ethnic policies, power struggles within the churches, and a problematic theology that highlighted concepts such as obedience to authority, while neglecting responsibility and love of the neighbor. At the same time, Schliesser points out that it is too simplistic to view all religious actors as equally implicated. Rather, the picture is more complex as numerous Church-led initiatives and individuals struggled for peace right up to the genocide.

MUSLIM PERSPECTIVE: RELIGION IN PAKISTAN'S INTERNAL CONFLICTS

Coming from a conflict resolution perspective, Muslim scholar S. Ayse Kadayifci-Orellana explores the relationship between religion and conflict within the context of Islamic tradition. More specifically, recognizing that Islam, like other religious traditions included in this book, embodies a dynamic and complex body of wisdom that is built on foundational resources such as the Quran and the Prophet's tradition, she investigates how groups like al-Qaeda and Taliban in Pakistan use and abuse Islamic tradition to justify violence and conflict. This section addresses: (1) conception of jihad in Islam from a historical and contemporary perspective, (2) the historical, social, and political context in which the Taliban and al-Qaeda emerged in Pakistan, and (3) how this context contributed to way these groups interpreted jihad to respond to modern social, political, and economic problems.

PART IV: RELIGION MATTERS IN CONFLICT RESOLUTION

ORIENTATION

Part IV is the sister of Part III. With Part III focusing on the conflictive side of religion, Part IV discusses religion's potent and often neglected constructive resources for conflict resolution and healing relationships. Our question here is: What are the potentials and specificities connected to religious peacemaking? What do religious actors have that others don't? Again, we first provide a general orientation to the topic by discussing the insights of recent scholarship (Schliesser 2019). While keeping in mind the vast diversity of religious actors in peacebuilding, certain specific characteristics emerge, both formal and content-based. Formal characteristics refer to competencies in building relationships, generating trust or being able to rely on extended and well-resourced networks. Content-based characteristics include certain concepts, for instance, the

Christian concepts of grace, forgiveness, and personal transformation or the Muslim concepts of mercy and doing good.

JEWISH PERSPECTIVE: RELIGION IN ISRAEL'S QUEST FOR CONFLICT RESOLUTION AND RECONCILIATION IN ITS LAND RIGHTS CONFLICTS

Reality demonstrates that religion has an ambivalent or dual nature, whereby it can be used to promote both peace and violence. Therefore, can Judaism contribute to resolving Israel's conflict over land with the Palestinians and its Arab citizens? Can a solution be found by relooking at the founding texts in the Hebrew Bible which demand peace, justice, and freedom for all which in contemporary Israel are concepts and values, identified in the 1948 Declaration of the Founding of the State of Israel, as key to how all its citizens—Jew and non-Jew—will be treated? Focusing on the work of two Israeli organizations, The Interreligious Coordinating Council in Israel and Rabbis for Human Rights, the role of religion in conflict resolution will be discussed in terms of their resources, methods, challenges, and achievements. This will be used to examine the potential of Jews to reclaim and assert the prophetic principles that combine to safeguard the existence and rights of people irrespective of race, ethnicity, or religion through compassion and empathetic understanding.

CHRISTIAN PERSPECTIVE: RELIGION IN POST-GENOCIDE RWANDA'S QUEST FOR CONFLICT RESOLUTION AND RECONCILIATION

With over 90 percent of the population adhering to the Christian faith, religious actors and especially Christian churches play a significant role in Rwanda's societal and political processes. Focusing on the Presbyterian Church of Rwanda, Schliesser traces the significance of religion in the government's official "National Politics of Reconciliation". The churches supplement the government's top-down strategies with bottom-up initiatives that are characterized by a focus on building long-term relationships, even with and between perpetrators and survivors and on disseminating Christian concepts such as forgiveness or grace. Next to the potentials apparent in the Christian churches' reconciliation efforts, certain problems surface. These include a problematic concept of justice, and a problematic culture of remembrance and silence on the state's human rights violations.

MUSLIM PERSPECTIVE: RELIGION IN MUSLIM WOMEN'S PEACEBUILDING INITIATIVES IN PAKISTAN

Following the 9/11 attacks, Islam has been often associated with violence and extremism. However, Islam, similar to other religious traditions, as a religion and a tradition is replete with teachings and practices of nonviolence and peacebuilding, and Muslims— both men and women—have been empowered by them to resolve their conflicts peacefully and to establish just social, political and economic systems (Kadayifci-Orellana 2007: 85). In this section, Kadayifci-Orellana will explore the often under-explored work of Muslim women who are employing these values and principles to address conflicts in their communities and to respond to challenges of violence. Focusing on the work of Mossarat Qadeem, founder of PAIMAN, an NGO working to respond to violence and radicalization of youth in Pakistan, Kadayifci-Orellana will explore how these Islamic principles of peace and justice inspire and create unique opportunities for Muslim women to build just and peaceful societies.

PART V: NOW WHAT?

From our key observation of religion matters in conflict and conflict resolution emerge a number of concrete implications. These include: Integration of religious actors (individuals, congregations, institutions, FBOs, etc., both local and trans-local) in conflict resolution; Establishment of advisory groups within a given body engaged in conflict resolution that include religious leaders and experts on the role of religion in societal processes; Promotion of religious literacy within a given body (political, academic, or NGO/ FBO) engaged in conflict resolution; Integration of women and youth in conflict resolution, for example through partnerships with local synagogues, churches, or mosques; Evaluation of religious peacebuilding work for better understanding its mechanisms, potentials, and problems.

REFERENCES

Appleby, R. Scott. (2000). *The Ambivalence of the Sacred: Religion, Violence and Reconciliation*. Lanham, MD: Rowman & Littlefield Publishers. doi.org/10.1177/106385120301200112

Berger, Julia. (2003). "Religious Non-Governmental Organizations: An Exploratory Analysis", *Voluntas: International Journal of Voluntary and Nonprofit Organizations,* 14(1): 15–39. doi.org/10.1023/A:1022988804887

Berger, Peter L. (ed.). (1999). *The Desecularization of the World. Resurgent Religion and World Politics*. Grand Rapids, MI: Eerdmans.

Council of the European Union. (2013). *EU Guidelines on the Promotion and Protection of Freedom of Religion or Belief*, Foreign Affairs Council meeting, Luxembourg, June 24, 2013, 1–18. Viewed from http://collections.internetmemory.org/haeu/content/20160313172652/http:/eeas.europa.eu/delegations/fiji/press_corner/all_news/news/2013/eu_guidelines_on_the_promotion_and_protection_of_freedom_of_religion_or_belief_%28june_24_2013_fac%29.pdf [Date accessed November 1, 2019].

Eisen, Robert. (2011). *The Peace and Violence of Judaism: From the Bible to Modern Zionism*. New York: Oxford University Press.

Frazer, Owen and Friedli, Richard. (2015). *Approaching Religion in Conflict Transformation: Concepts, Cases and Practical Implications*, Center for Security Studies (CSS), ETH Zurich. Viewed from www.css.ethz.ch/content/dam/ethz/special-interest/gess/cis/center-for-securities-studies/pdfs/Approaching-Religion-In-Conflict-Transformation2.pdf [Date accessed November 1, 2019].

Frazer, Owen and Owen, Mark. (2018). *Religion in Conflict and Peacebuilding: Analysis Guide*. Washington, DC, United States Institute of Peace. Viewed from www.usip.org/sites/default/files/USIP_Religion-in-Conflict-Peacebuilding_Analysis-Guide.pdf [Date accessed November 1, 2019].

Freeman, Dena. (2012). "The Pentecostal Ethic and the Spirit of Development", in Dena Freeman (ed.), *Pentecostalism and Development. Churches, NGOs and Social Change in Africa*. New York: Palgrave Macmillan, 1–38.

Galtung, Johan. (1969). "Violence, Peace and Peace Research", *Journal of Peace Research,* 6: 167–191. doi.org/10.1177/002234336900600301

Guterres, António. (2017). *Guterres Highlights Importance of Recognizing the Links Between Peace and Sustainable Development*. Viewed from www.un.org/sustainabledevelopment/blog/2017/01/guterres-highlights-importance-of-recognizing-the-links-between-peace-and-sustainable-development/ [Date accessed November 1, 2019].

Kadayifci-Orellana, S. Ayse. (2007). *Standing on an Isthmus: Islamic Approaches to War and Peace in Palestine*. Lanham, MD: Lexington Books.

Kriesberg, Louis. (2009). "The Evolution of Conflict Resolution", in Jacob Bercovitch, Victor Kremenyuk, and I. William Zartman (eds.), *The SAGE Handbook of Conflict Resolution*. Los Angeles: Sage, 15–32. doi.org/10.4135/9780857024701

Pew Research Center. (2015). *The Future of World Religions: Population Growth Projections, 2010–2050*. Viewed from www.pewforum.org/2015/04/02/religious-projections-2010–2050/ [Date accessed November 1, 2019].

Schliesser, Christine. (2019). "Conflict Resolution and Peacebuilding", in Jeffrey Haynes (ed.), *Routledge Handbook of Religion and Political Parties*. London: Routledge, 126–138.

Waardenburg, Jacques. (1986). *Religionen und Religion. Systematische Einführung in die Religionswissenschaft*. Berlin: De Gruyter.

PART III
RELIGION MATTERS IN CONFLICT

3

ORIENTATION
DID RELIGION DO IT?

Christine Schliesser,
S. Ayse Kadayifci-Orellana,
and Pauline Kollontai

RELIGION AND VIOLENCE: BEST FRIENDS FOREVER?

When we look at human history, both past and present, religion and violence appear to be best friends. While religiously inspired violence is nothing new, the events surrounding 9/11 have brought them sharply to the forefront of the Western world. Ever since, religious violence has been considered one of the most pressing issues of our times (cf. Juergensmeyer 2017). This perception is backed by numbers as the past decade has seen a substantial increase in violent religious tensions. "Religious ideologies and commitment are indisputably central factors in the escalation of violence and evil around the world" (Kimball 2008: 4). According to a recent report by the Pew Research Center (Pew Research Center 2018), more than one-quarter of the world's countries experience high or very high levels of social hostilities involving religion, compared to one-fifth in 2007. At the same time, government restrictions on religion continue to climb, as does the harassment of most religious groups. There are, however, some problems connected with the term "religious violence". For one, it might be misunderstood as if religion was the primary or even sole force behind violence. Rather, roots of conflicts entail other dimensions as well, for instance, political, economic or social reasons. Second, the term religious violence can lead to a problematic legitimation of violence by implying that religious violence is always irrational and fanatical and must be defeated by secular violence which is in turn rational and controlled (Cavanaugh 2004).

With much of academic and popular attention still focusing on the violent sides of religion, scholars such as R. Scott Appleby (2000), Marc Gopin (2012; 2000) and Robert Eisen (2011) have emphasized the inherent ambiguity of religion. Religion and violent conflict can indeed seem like best friends, but so can religion and conflict resolution or reconciliation. While Part IV of this book engages with the constructive sides of religion in building peace and reconciliation, Part III focuses on how religion can actually fuel violence and conflict. For before we can attempt to engage religion for conflict resolution and peacemaking, we need to understand how religion functions in conflicts with religious dimensions. There are different models available that can help us understand better the roles of religion in conflict. We have found the works of Owen Frazer, Richard Friedli, and Mark Owen, all academic-practitioners connected to policy-making, very helpful as they differentiate between different ways of approaching religion within conflicts (Frazer and Owen 2018; Frazer and Friedli 2015). Below, we combine their work.

RELIGION AND VIOLENCE (BRIEFLY) REVISITED

Our study takes into account that "no universally accepted definition of religion or faith exists" (Ware, Ware, and Clarke 2016: 324). Rather than engaging in discussions around substantial versus functional definitions of religion, we proceed from the pragmatic premise to understand "religion" as what is described as "religion" by interlocutors and communities in a given context (Waardenburg 1986). As for the analysis of religion in situations of conflict, Frazer and Friedli point us to three factors that shape our understanding (Frazer and Friedli 2015: 9). First, the nature and role of religion in society. Religion has no existence in and of itself but always takes shape in a particular time and context. The role religion plays in a given conflict is therefore connected to the role it plays in the society in which the conflict takes place. Second, the relevance of different dimensions of religion in a specific conflict. Due to the fact that there are many dimensions of religion in a given society, their respective influence on a conflict differs. Third, the individual understanding of religion by the analyst him- or herself. No perspective is ever entirely neutral or objective. This holds especially true in the field of religion and conflict. The analyst's personal view on religion is therefore likely to have some influence on how the role of religion is understood in a certain conflict.

While conflict itself can be both constructive and destructive, violence is always destructive. Violence, according to Johan Galtung, can manifest at three interrelated levels, namely: the direct, structural, and cultural levels (Galtung 1990). At the direct level, perpetrator and victim can often be directly identified. Perpetrators (and victims), however, have often interiorized violent structures that can function as a latent, underlying trigger of personal violence. Any kind of discrimination, for example, would fall into this category of structural violence, as well as the unjust distribution of resources and opportunities. In order to justify their violent actions—explicitly or implicitly—perpetrators often resort to foundational narratives that are part of the cultural dimension of violence. Here, Galtung speaks of "deep culture" (*Tiefenkultur*) that provides the legitimation of violence through respective traditions. Deep cultures are nourished by cultural memories, by foundational narratives and by systems of value. Next to these three factors, other aspects that need to be considered include unjust economic structures, mass media influences, climatic conditions, or psychological conditions created, for instance, by charismatic leaders. Furthermore, attention needs to be given to the roots of violence. Here, René Girard's thoughts on the mimetic nature of violence are very helpful. Human conflict, according to Girard, is rooted in desire and rivalry rather than in differences of opinion or ideology and can easily escalate in a spiral of violence that needs a scapegoat in order to be stopped (Girard 2008; Hodge, Cowdell, Fleming, and Osborn 2018).

RELIGION IN CONFLICTS: SIX WAYS TO THINK ABOUT ITS ROLE(S)

Much of conflict analysis tends to view religion as either irrelevant, and hence neglectable, or too complex to be of any use, thus relegating it to the realm of specialists. Neither approach is satisfactory. The first is blind to a significant factor both in conflict and conflict resolution. The latter neglects the fact that religion is in fact connected to many different dimensions of a given conflict. Gaining a precise understanding of the roles of religion in conflict is crucial for developing effective approaches for conflict resolution. In order to shed light on the ominous "religious factor" in conflict, Friedli, Frazer, and Owen identify the following six ways of thinking about religion in conflict by way of analyzing different case studies. These include understanding religion as community, as a set of teachings, as spirituality, as practice, as discourse, and as an institution (Frazer and Owen 2018: 10; Frazer and Friedli 2015: 10). Just like religion in general, each aspect is ambiguous in and of itself and can serve as a source of conflict or as a resource for conflict resolution. These six ways of understanding religion are not mutually exclusive, in that any number of them might have an impact in any given context. The aspects are fuzzy on the edges, meaning that there is some overlap with others. In the following sections, we will introduce each aspect, using different examples to illustrate the practical implications of it for conflict analysis and, subsequently, conflict resolution. We also point to helpful questions to ask when analyzing the roles of religion in a conflict (Frazer and Friedli 2015: 28).

RELIGION AS COMMUNITY: AUTHORITIES, RELATIONSHIPS, AND IDENTITIES

According to French sociologist Émile Durkheim (1858–1917), religion is "a unified system of beliefs and practices relative to sacred things, that is to say, things set apart and forbidden—beliefs and practices which unite into one single moral community called a Church, all those who adhere to them" (Durkheim 1915: 47). Next to other aspects, this definition emphasizes the community-building, integrative dimension of religion. The structural functionalist school of Durkheim and his followers were interested in the way religion serves to create and uphold societal structures and institutions, for instance, the family and the state. This includes the legitimation of authorities, the respective roles of men and women, as well as the sanctions rendered against those who act contrary to these structures. In conflict situations, this community-forming aspect of religion can be both divisive and constructive. It can be used to forcefully uphold traditional authorities and to suppress deviant voices. Yet it can also be a resource for building relationships and social cohesion, even beyond group boundaries, and strengthening community resilience.

Next to religion's role in constituting authorities and power structures, this perspective points to religion's impact on identity formation. Religion is a powerful source for establishing identities, both on personal and collective levels. Again, this dimension is ambivalent. It can serve to form alliances by connecting people of the same religion even across otherwise separating identities, such as along ethnic or national lines. Yet by establishing an "us", religion can also create a "them", thereby engaging in divisive "othering". Many current brands of religio-nationalist identity, such as Hindu nationalism in India or Buddhist nationalism in Sri Lanka, play off this powerful dimension of religion. The Northern-Irish conflict (1969–1998) also centered strongly on religion as community and as identity marker. The terms "Protestant" or "Catholic" served not only as religious labels, but included social, political, and economic aspects, as each group drew its identity to a large extent through separating oneself from the perceived "other". At the same time, the peace process benefitted not least from the cross-community relationship and trust building across religious actors like the Methodist minister Harold Good and Catholic priest Alec Reid, who were selected as the two independent witnesses overseeing the decommissioning of IRA arms after the 1998 Good Friday Agreement.

For the analysis of the role of religion in a conflict and for creating possible entry points for conflict resolution, questions to ask include: Do religious identities serve to divide communities? Is there a shared religious identity that could serve to connect people across conflict lines? How can religious actors and institutions build relationships between people and reduce tension?

RELIGION AS A SET OF TEACHINGS: CONCEPTS, NORMS, AND VALUES

Different from the "functional" perspective on religion apparent above, "substantial" views focus on the content of a religion, its set of teachings or doctrines. For the Abrahamic religions, their Holy Scriptures—the Torah, the Bible, and the Quran—are of crucial importance because they are viewed as containing divine revelation. While other religions are less focused on sacred texts, religious teachings are nevertheless important in most traditions. They not only help religious teachings to make sense of life, they also often include distinctive norms and values for everyday behavior. Through their ethical implications, religions can contribute to a shared understanding of norms and laws, thereby increasing social cohesion. At the same time, this entails a danger of othering, if, for example, the Sharia law is used to create boundaries between "us" (the believers) vs. "them" (the unbelievers).

Again, religious teachings are ambiguous. They can be used as effective weapons in inciting violence and conflict, yet they are equally powerful tools for peace and reconciliation. Both religious peacemakers and religious suicide bombers refer to their Holy Scriptures in order to explain their actions. In his study of Judaism, Robert Eisen traces major Jewish texts from the Bible to modern Zionism and shows how each of these texts can be used for teachings on peace and on violence (Eisen 2011). With reference to the Bible, for example, Eisen sees three sources of ambiguity:

> ambiguity in the semantic meaning of the biblical text, from the smallest to the largest units, ambiguity in the relative weight given to particular phrases, passages, or concepts within the overall scheme of the Bible; and ambiguity regarding the use of historical context to explain violent passages.
>
> (Eisen 2011: 64)

How these texts are read and understood, Eisen points out, depends on the complex interplay between religious traditions and forces from the outside such as from politics, society, and economy.

At the same time, the interreligious search for common ground and shared values, such as peace or justice, has proven a potent tool in the reduction of stereotypes and interreligious tensions. The Jordan-based initiative "A Common Word Between Us and You", for example, launched a seminal Muslim-Christian dialogue in 2007 based on the concepts of loving God and neighbor. This ongoing interfaith dialogue project has received positive reactions from Christian, Muslim, and Jewish leaders worldwide and continues to contribute to interfaith cooperation.

Questions to ask in the analysis of religion's role in a conflict and for seeking ways to transform the conflict include: How are religious teachings being used to ignite and justify conflictive behavior? How are they used to promote peace and reconciliation? How are religious teachings being used to identify common ground between conflict parties?

RELIGION AS SPIRITUALITY: PERSONAL EXPERIENCE, MOTIVATION, AND MEANING

Spirituality refers to personal experiences of faith and bestows a sense of motivation and meaning. Spirituality often plays out in a particular lifestyle and in certain ethical choices, individually or as part of community life, such as in a religious order, ashram, or Sufi circle. In conflict situations, experiences of spirituality can act as a strong motivator, in particular in combination with experiences of meaning or purpose. Violent Muslim extremists, for example, have justified their attacks with reference to their understanding of doing God's will (Kruglanski et al. 2009). Here, the eschatological framework of many religions plays a crucial role. The individual person sees him- or herself as embedded in a larger framework that even extends beyond the boundaries of death and time. One's own individual and finite life becomes thereby connected to a bigger purpose and meaning. Not only does the spiritual dimension of religion serve as a potent motivator for specific actions—both conflictive and constructive—common spiritual experiences can also help create strong bonds between people, even across lines, furthering both in-group and out-group experiences.

The activities of the NGO International Center for Religion and Diplomacy (ICRD) during the Kashmir conflict 2000–2007 provide an example of approaching religion in conflict through the perspective of religion as spirituality. Working with a conflict resolution framework called "Faith-Based Reconciliation", ICRD promotes the idea that the three Abrahamic religions share the principles of pluralism, social justice, forgiveness, and God's sovereignty (Cox 2007).

For the Kashmir context, this approach was modified to include non-Abrahamic traditions, for example, references to Gandhian non-violence. In their faith-based reconciliation seminars, ICRD brought together next-generation leaders from all strands of Kashmiri society, including religion, civil society, business, or media, and from all main religious groups. During the seminars, participants not only formed relationships across boundaries, but were also invited to participate in religious rituals including prayers, reading of religious texts, and speaking words of apology and forgiveness.

In analyzing the role of religion in a conflict, the following questions help in discerning its spiritual dimension and in creating points of entry for conflict transformation: How are shared spiritual experiences used to strengthen exclusive group identities or, respectively, to create connections between people? What divisive or peace-promoting behavior do actors explain as motivated by their spiritual experiences?

RELIGION AS PRACTICE: SYMBOLS AND RITUALS

It is in practice that religion becomes visible. Dress, food, and certain forms of behavior, for example, towards the poor, and different rituals, are part of religion as practice. Weeks, years, and life cycles are being structured by the rhythm of religion. Traditionally, religion plays a significant role in *rites de passage* (Van Gennep 2004) as it guides through the hazards of life's transitions. Birth, entering adulthood, marriage, and death mark turning points in life. In sacralized codes and rituals, religion provides stability, structure, and meaning through these perilous passages, thereby re-enacting and preserving the socially constructed world. Catholic Christianity, for instance, knows of different sacraments throughout the life cycle, including baptism, confirmation, marriage, and the anointment of the sick. Furthermore, through the participation in rituals, from Sunday service over circumcision to pilgrimages, such as *haddsh*, social bonds are being formed and strengthened. While relationships may be created even beyond boundaries, symbols and rituals can also serve to enforce in-group and out-group identities.

In the context of conflict, religion as practice plays out in several respects. For one, practices themselves can become matters of contestation, thereby fueling conflict. For example, the relationships between Japan, on the one hand, and China and South Korea, on the other, have been repeatedly tried by the visits of Japanese officials to the Yasukuni Shrine. This Shinto shrine is dedicated to the commemoration of those who died in service of Japan, including convicted war criminals. Visits by high-ranking officials are therefore perceived and criticized by China and South Korea as displaying a problematic view of history on the side of Japan and as belittlement of Japan's war crimes. Other examples of religious practices contributing to conflict include the blessing of swords and other weaponry. The ritual of *benedictio armorum* was performed by the churches and enjoyed high popularity in the Middle Ages. Yet religion as practice can also yield significant resources for coping with conflict. Times of conflict are intensely unsettling, during which familiar rituals and ceremonies provide much-needed structure and comfort. Even more so, they may be used to facilitate helpful rites of passages that constructively deal with the past, such as through reconciliation rituals and commemoration ceremonies. Here, traditional rituals may be used and adapted, or new rituals may be created as the case study of Rwanda shows (Chapter 9).

Questions to ask for conflict analysis and resolution include: What practices are sources of division? What practices help to overcome barriers and to build relationships?

RELIGION AS DISCOURSE: LANGUAGE, POWER, AND *WELTANSCHAUUNG*

With the other four ways of approaching religion focusing on one specific aspect of religion, such as practices, or teachings, religion as discourse is the most comprehensive perspective. Discourse in this sense refers, initially, to the specific vocabularies and languages used for communication. In the context of conflict, this has a twofold significance. On the one hand, contestation can refer to the acknowledgment of the legitimacy of different interpretations. Recent studies point to a correlation between conflict and allowing or not allowing for different meanings of a term (Ochs et al. 2018). On the other hand, acknowledging diverse interpretations is only the first step. Different interpretations can themselves become a source of tensions, for instance, when the term "justice" is used in diverse ways by various parties. Efforts in "translations" are needed in order to facilitate genuine communication.

Yet religion as discourse goes beyond mere semantics. Michel Foucault points us to the fact that discourse is an entire system that includes language, but also thought, practices, and ideas. These systems are subject to constellations of power and knowledge. Religion as discourse thus means the social construction of reality and how it is perceived, a whole *Weltanschauung* with its own internal logic. Along similar lines, George Lindbeck (1984: 33) defines religion as "a kind of cultural and/or linguistic framework or medium that shapes the entirety of life and thought". This framework is a dynamic construct and set in the context of constant power struggles, both internally and externally. By internal power struggles we mean conflicts within a religious tradition, for instance, regarding authoritative interpretations of certain norms or Scripture passages. External power struggles, on the other hand, point to the fact that religious systems are not disconnected from the world, but are always part of larger political, economic, and social dynamics. In conflict situations, tensions can revolve around the incommensurability of different discourses. This results in communication problems when particular concepts, for instance of a secular state separating religion and politics, only make sense from within a certain framework. Often, the acceptance of certain statements within a discourse depends on those who are perceived to speak in authority. Their authority can give legitimacy to both conflictive and constructive language and behavior. Just as some Catholic priests condoned and practiced ethnic hatred and violence during the genocide in Rwanda, thereby inciting other Christians, figures like Archbishop Emeritus Desmond Tutu proved a powerful example of reconciliation rather than revenge in post-apartheid South Africa.

Helpful questions when approaching religion as discourse include: What are the differing worldviews behind opposing discourses? Do problems of interpretation contribute to tensions? How can different understandings be translated to facilitate genuine dialogue?

RELIGION AS AN INSTITUTION: LEADERS, NETWORKS, AND SERVICE DELIVERY

Religion is institutionalized at different levels, extending from the local congregation over regional and national councils to international networks. Religious institutions are engaged in the delivery of a variety of services, including worship, education, and health. Through their leaders, religion receives visibility and a "face" (for instance, Ayatollah Khomeini in Iran and Archbishop Emeritus Desmond Tutu in South Africa). By means of their leadership and the hierarchy they represent, religious institutions can be powerful agents for both conflict and conflict resolution. Recent conflict analysis has found the intermediate level of leadership particularly influential as it connects to both the grassroot level and higher authorities. At the same time, religious leadership is still mostly dominated by older men, while women are at times systematically excluded. The Buddhist Sangha in Thailand, for instance, refuses to accept women's ordination. The same holds true for the Catholic Church, some Protestant denominations, and many Muslim and Jewish congregations.

In terms of conflict resolution, religious institutions can be helpful for creating a platform for advocacy and raising awareness. Due to their local, regional, and even international links, they can often-times access financial, logistical, and human resources. For external parties, such as UN peacekeeping forces, religious institutions can become valuable contacts with insider knowledge of the context, the conflict, and its religious dimensions. With their influence and mobilization powers, religious institutions can provide important support to peace processes. The Inter-Religious Council of Sierra Leone (IRCSL) is an example of approaching the institutional dimension of religion in the transformation of a conflict. In 1991, civil war erupted between the government and the rebel group RUF (Revolutionary United Front). In 1997, nine Muslim and 19 Christian leaders formed the IRCSL to advocate for dialogue and the end of violence. Through their joint commitment, they managed to rally public support for peace, thus pressuring both the government and the rebels to end the conflict. Their effort contributed significantly to the Lomé Peace Accords of 1999.

Questions to approach religion as an institution in conflict analysis include: In what ways are religious institutions part of the conflict? Which engagements are divisive, and which promote peace?

In this chapter, we focused on the conflictive dimensions of religion and asked: Did religion do it? By ways of unpacking the complexities of "religious violence", we discussed six different ways of approaching religion in conflicts: religion as community, as a set of teachings, as spirituality, as practice, as discourse, and as an institution. This orientation will be followed by three case studies, spelling out the concrete implications of religion in different conflicts, namely, in Israel, Rwanda, and Pakistan.

REFERENCES

Appleby, R. Scott. (2000). *The Ambivalence of the Sacred: Religion, Violence and Reconciliation*. Lanham, MD: Rowman & Littlefield.

Cavanaugh, William T. (2004). "Sins of Omission: What 'Religion and Violence' Arguments Ignore", *The Hedgehog Review: Critical Reflections on Contemporary Culture*, 6(1): 34–50.

Cox, Brian. (2007). *Faith-Based Reconciliation: A Moral Vision That Transforms People and Societies*. Bloomington, IN: Xlibris Corporation.

Durkheim, Émile. (1915). *The Elementary Forms of Religious Life* (trans. by J.W. Swain). London: Allen & Unwin.

Eisen, Robert. (2011). *The Peace and Violence of Judaism: From the Bible to Modern Zionism*. Oxford: Oxford University Press.

Frazer, Owen and Friedli, Richard. (2015). *Approaching Religion in Conflict Transformation: Concepts, Cases and Practical Implications*, Center for Security Studies (CSS), ETH Zurich. Viewed from www.css.ethz.ch/content/dam/ethz/special-interest/gess/cis/center-for-securities-studies/pdfs/Approaching-Religion-In-Conflict-Transformation2.pdf [Date accessed November 1, 2019].

Frazer, Owen and Owen, Mark. (2018). *Religion in Conflict and Peacebuilding: Analysis Guide*, Washington, DC: United States Institute of Peace. Viewed from www.usip.org/sites/default/files/USIP_Religion-in-Conflict-Peacebuilding_Analysis-Guide.pdf [Date accessed November 1, 2019].

Galtung, Johan. (1990). "Cultural Violence", *Journal of Peace Research*, 27(3): 291–305.

Girard, René. (2008). *Violence and the Sacred*. London: Athlone.

Gopin, Marc. (2000). *Between Eden and Armageddon: The Future of World Religions, Violence and Peacemaking*. New York: Oxford University Press.

Gopin, Marc. (2012). *Bridges Across an Impossible Divide: The Inner Lives of Arab and Jewish Peacemakers*. Oxford: Oxford University Press.

Hodge, Joel, Cowdell, Scott, Fleming, Chris, and Osborn, Carly. (eds.) (2018). *Does Religion Cause Violence? Multidisciplinary Perspectives on Violence and Religion in the Modern World*. London: Bloomsbury Academic.

Juergensmeyer, Mark. (2017). *Terror in the Mind of God. The Global Rise of Religious Violence* (4th ed.). Oakland: University of California Press.

Kimball, Charles. (2008). *When Religion Becomes Evil* (rev. ed.). San Francisco: HarperOne.

Kruglanski, Arie W. Chen, Xiaoyan, Dechesne, Mark, Fishman, Shira, and Orehek, Edward. (2009). "Fully Committed: Suicide Bombers' Motivation and the Quest for Personal Significance", *Political Psychology,* 30: 341–344. https://doi.org/10.1111/j.1467-9221.2009.00698.x

Lindbeck, George. (1984). *The Nature of Doctrine: Religion and Theology in a Postliberal Age.* Philadelphia, PA: Westminster Press.

Ochs, Peter, Faizi, Nauman, Teubner, Jonathan, and Moulvi, Zain. (2018). "Value Predicate Analysis: A Language-Based Tool for Diagnosing Behavioral Tendencies of Religious or Value-Based Groups in Region of Conflict", *Journal for the Scientific Study of Religion,* 58(1): 1–21. doi.org/10.1111/jssr.12574

Pew Research Center. (2018). *Global Uptick in Government Restrictions on Religion in 2016.* Viewed from www.pewforum.org/2018/06/21/global-uptick-in-government-restrictions-on-religion-in-2016/ [Date accessed November 1, 2019].

Van Gennep, Arnold. (2004). *The Rites of Passage.* London: Routledge.

Waardenburg, Jacques. (1986). *Religionen und Religion. Systematische Einführung in die Religionswissenschaft.* Berlin: de Gruyter.

Ware, Vicki-Ann, Ware, Anthony, and Clarke, Matthew. (2016). "Domains of Faith Impact: How 'Faith' is Perceived to Shape Faith-Based International Development Organisations", *Development in Practice,* 26(3): 321–333.

JEWISH PERSPECTIVE
RELIGION IN ISRAEL'S LAND RIGHTS CONFLICTS

Pauline Kollontai

INTRODUCTION

On November 29, 1947, the United Nations General Assembly voted to partition Palestine into a Jewish and an Arab state. While the Jewish community agreed to the proposed partition and allocation of territory, the Palestinian Arabs did not, calling the UN declaration of the State of Israel "al-Nakba", the catastrophe. Despite the non-agreement of the Palestinian Arabs the establishment of the State of Israel took place in May 1948. Israel is identified as being both Jewish and democratic in its Founding Declaration of Establishment. The Declaration states that Jews have a historical right to this land because it was "the birthplace of the Jewish people where their spiritual, religious and political identity was shaped" (Ben-Gurion 1948: 1). The values of justice, freedom, and peace are identified in the Declaration as being rooted in the traditions of the Hebrew Prophets and a commitment is given to practicing these through social, political, and religious rights for all citizens of Israel.

This case study discusses the role of the Jewish tradition in the ongoing tensions and violence in Israel's conflict over territory as evidenced internally in the Negev concerning Bedouin land rights and externally with Palestinian territory. The discussion here will draw on aspects derived from Frazer, Friedli, and Owen's understanding of the role of religion in conflict and reconciliation which we outlined earlier in this book (Frazer and Friedli 2015; Frazer and Owen 2018, cf. Chapter 3).

ORIGINS AND CONTEXT OF THE WAR OVER LAND

The dominant issue in Israel's existence since 1948 has been land with the Palestinians. By 1949 Israel had already expanded unlawfully into Palestinian territory during the War of Independence (1947–1949) with Palestinian Arabs and Arabs from neighboring countries. Over 6,000 Israelis were killed and 15,000 wounded (IMFA n.d.: 1). By the time of the armistice in 1949, the Israelis had extended their territory at the cost of 750,000 Palestinians who fled or were forcibly driven from their homes (UNCCP 1950). Over 5,000 Arab combatants died (this included 3,700 Arabs from outside Palestine) and over 11,000 Palestinian civilians were missing or presumed dead (Morris 2008: 404–406). The taking of more land by Israel from Syria, Jordan and Egypt occurred during the Six-Day War (1967) and the Yom Kippur War (1972). Israel has continued to control and/or occupy parts of the Palestinian territories, which has included the building of Jewish settlements in the West Bank. Palestinian response to the ongoing situation is seen through the first and second intifadas and the use of suicide bombers.

Other expressions of the land struggle are evident through Israel's border controls, checkpoints, and the building of the West Bank Wall. At a total length of 440 miles there are points where it has cut over 11 miles into the West Bank, thereby violating the United Nations "Green Line" agreed in the original signing of the resolution of the State of Israel in 1947. The incursion of the wall into Palestinian territory has affected over 25,000 Palestinians either by finding themselves now living in Israel or sometimes finding parts of their property or land split between Palestine and Israel (UN OCHA 2011). Building on the wall commenced in June 2002 and was announced as one of Israel's security and defense measures against Palestinian suicide bombers whose acts by 2002 had killed 553 people and injured 645 people. The majority of the dead or injured were Israeli citizens and not military or police personnel. Given the reality of the consequences of the acts of suicide bombings there was an urgent need for Israel to find a way to try and end these attacks. The solution was to build the wall. But building this wall has only provided part of the solution—it has significantly reduced the number of suicide bombing attacks since 2003. But it has not addressed the central issue for the Palestinians of having their own independent state. The wall reinforces fear, suspicion, and hatred on both sides.

The other main land conflict in Israel is with the Negev Bedouin who are Israeli citizens. The majority of Bedouin in Israel who live in the Negev are from tribes who in the 18th and 19th centuries came from the Arabian Peninsula. In 1947 about 65,000–90,000 Bedouins lived in the Negev under British rule (Marx 1967: 3). Following the establishment of the State of Israel in May 1948, the Israeli Defense Forces (IDF) took most of the Negev from the Egyptians between October and December 1948. During this time, most of the Bedouin left the Negev, large numbers of them moving to Sinai, the Hebron mountains, or areas around the Dead Sea. By 1953 around 11,000 Bedouin lived in the Negev and were under Military Administration until 1966. As the troubles subsided, some Bedouin returned to the area where either they were allowed to stay and live in the eastern plain of Be'er Sheva or they were expelled by the Military Administration. The 1960 census shows that the number of Bedouin in the Negev had risen slightly to 16,000 and that 6,700 were living in Galilee (Marx 1967: 3). The use of a military administration after the cessation of these initial hostilities in the Negev had a serious impact on the experience of those Bedouins who returned. The ongoing Israeli policy is to reject the majority of Bedouin land claims; instead Bedouin have to rent their land from the state. There are also two categories assigned to Bedouin villages—recognized and unrecognized villages. For those Bedouin who refuse to recognize the state as the owners of their ancestral lands and continue to live in "unrecognized villages", the state continues to offer them alternative land to live on so that the state can use their existing land for other purposes. Continuing refusal to move usually results in the bulldozing down of Bedouin homes and property. During the 1960s and 1970s some Bedouin were moved to government-built towns as part of Israel's urbanization and resettlement strategy of the Negev Bedouin. But these towns have not been that successful in integrating Bedouin into Israeli society and providing equality of access to social and public services. Instead, they have to some extent ghettoized Bedouin into enclaves where they continue to be separated from their Jewish neighbors and have been neglected in terms of infrastructure and services and have high unemployment and crime rates (Swirski and Hasson 2006: 87).

The conflict over Bedouin land is part of a wider government agenda to "Judaise" the Negev. The vision of Judaising the Negev to the extent planned has been greatly encouraged and supported in Haredi and Orthodox Jewish communities throughout Israel. The Negev Bedouin are considered by many Israelis as a barrier to realizing this vision. There is a twofold approach which the Israeli state has employed since the late 1950s. First, to assimilate Bedouin into types of citizens acceptable to the Israeli state which requires a diminishing of their religious, ethnic, and cultural identities and practices. A tool to try and achieve this has been by state funding for targeted economic and welfare investment for individuals, families, and communities who show compliance with the state's agenda. Second, Bedouin who continue to challenge the state on land rights usually face a lack of state resources in terms of social infrastructure regarding their living environment and also in educational, welfare, and health provision.

RELIGION AS COMMUNITY: IDENTITY, AUTHORITIES, AND RELATIONSHIPS

According to context and interaction with other identity-forming elements (language, ethnicity, politics, and culture), religious belief systems "can have a particular identity-forming potential. Religion tells you where you belong, what to believe and where to proceed" (Harpviken and Roislien 2005: 9). Religion is social in character, offering the individual a sense of belonging to a community of believers who share beliefs, rituals, and places of historical and religious importance and relevance in contemporary life and experience. An example of a place combining religious and historical importance is Masada in Southern Israel, the site of the Jews' last stand against the Romans after the fall of Jerusalem in 70 CE. The events at Masada are described "as a pivotal moment in Jewish history – one of perseverance, bravery and commitment … [Masada] became a symbol of courage for the young modern Jewish state as it … struggled for survival" (Rosenbaum 2019: 1). The memory and significance of Masada continues to be invoked in the context of Israel's survival today with the most recent project "Inscribing the Jewish Future on Masada", set up by the American branch of the Jewish National Fund (JNF) and fully supported by the Israeli government. This new initiative builds on a project started in 2008 which enabled a Torah scribe to be present on a daily basis in the rebuilt Geniza room, part of the ancient Masada synagogue, where visitors had the opportunity to watch him at work. In 2019 this project continues to enable visitors to watch the scribe at work and now they can pay for one letter, a word, a sentence, a verse, a section, or even a whole Torah. In return they are given a certificate confirming that they have contributed to the writing of a Torah scroll. Completed scrolls are dedicated and donated to those Jewish communities in Israel, such as the Kibbutz Kerem Shalom near the Gaza border, which in recent years have been hit by rockets fired by Hamas. Attending the Torah dedication ceremony at the kibbutz was a member of JNF's National Community Campaign James Riola, who said,

> I looked around the kibbutz and within 100 feet of where we were standing was a 30-foot wall. It struck me that on the other side of the wall there was such violence, but on this side of the wall where we had the Torah, everyone was so happy and excited.

> (Rosenbaum 2019: 1)

Religion can serve as a link with nationhood and can provide non-religious events of the state with a sense of transcendence as seen with the example of the annual Founding of the State of Israel celebrations. Religion can nurture and sustain nationalism, which in its more negative expression can dehumanize, expel, or destroy those considered as "outsiders" within a nation-state. Religion, to varying degrees and in various historical contexts, is from time to time a conduit for characteristics of tribalism. Religious identity can be on a variant between inclusive and exclusive. Judaism initially emerges with a model of God that is tribal in the way He chooses His people, the Israelites, and makes them into a nation through violence and war towards other peoples, whether justifiable or not. Religion, which expresses the concept and values of tribalism and exclusivism, diminishes the possibility of social trust, cohesion, and collective solidarity, and can lead to violation of the Golden Rule principle which is intended to facilitate respect, empathy, and unity amongst people in diverse contexts. Since its founding in 1948, there is evidence to show the ongoing negative influence of the Haredi and Orthodox Jewish communities in the Israeli body politics' approach to conflict between Jews and non-Jews in Israel, and with the Palestinians in the Israeli controlled territories of Palestine.

RELIGION AS A SET OF TEACHINGS AND PRACTICE: TRIBAL GOD, LAND, AND VIOLENCE

Religion can provide a system of meaning and a framework for action. It constitutes a normative system which, "when accepted, serves as a directive for how each individual believer should live their life" through following the laws, command, and teachings of a divine transcendent being (Harpviken and Roislen 2005: 8). The cognitive aspect of this normative system is that it can shape the individuals' world views, which are then further shaped by aspects and experiences of their social contexts, both past and present. The degree to which the religious system of meaning is closed or open will affect the individual's understanding and response to situations of diversity, difference, and potential for survival. In the case of Israel and its establishment in the aftermath of the Holocaust, religion and culture is shaped in the context of Jewish survival, security, and continuity. The issue of land is essential to all three of these. The importance of land in the Israeli Jewish public consciousness, especially Haredi and Orthodox Jews, is found in the concept of "a promised land" given by God to his people following their exodus and liberation from slavery in Egypt during biblical times. Having a land of one's own provides more likelihood of peace and freedom, of being safe and secure. But as the Jewish scriptures show, this was not always the case, as foreign armies attacked Israel at various times, sometimes exiling the Israelites or occupying their land. In turn, Israel also engaged in campaigns to extend its territory by taking land from other people. God's gift of a promised land to Israel was already the land of other people, the Canaanites.

The historical narrative of the land as being God-given to the Jewish people has led to a growth in religious violence carried out by Jewish extremist groups, typically made up of youth from the

Haredi and Orthodox communities in Israel, since 2010 (BDHRL 2011). These groups see nothing wrong in committing violence most certainly towards non-Jewish Israeli citizens, but also sometimes against Jews not considered truly Jews (Reform and Liberal), and on other occasions against Israeli soldiers for being "too soft" on Israel's non-Jewish population and Palestinians in the Palestinian Territories, "It is legitimized, motivated, and guided by a religious code. It draws, in a powerful way, the boundaries between them and the 'others'" (Nachman 2010: 174). The key issue driving their violence is the belief that Israel is the land which God gave to his chosen people and not to anyone else. Their theological understanding of the Promised Land has fused with a form of Israeli nationalism which is exclusivist as regards the Jewish right to the land of Israel. Of course, the use of violence by some Jews based on their understanding of Jewish teaching is not a new invention and some of the Israeli Jewish leadership either promote or ignore their members' acts of religious violence. Indeed, some religious leaders actively promote religious violence. One example is Rabbi Yosef Elitzur Fein, a rabbi in a West Bank settlement, who posted social media advocating incitement to violence against Palestinians and Israeli soldiers and is also co-author of a controversial book, *The King's Torah*, that attempts to provide religious justification for the killing of non-Jews. Eventually, in December 2016, an Israeli court sentenced him to five months' community service for the social media posts calling for violent acts against Palestinians and Israeli soldiers (BDHRL 2017: 43). Another example of this extremism is of "Price tag" attacks, also known as "Mutual Responsibility", which are acts of vandalism carried out by Jewish fundamentalist settler youths against the property of Palestinians, Christians, and left-wing Israeli Jews.

Enforcing Jewish ownership of land is reflected in the recent adoption of the Nation State Law by Israel's parliament in July 2018. In this new law Israel is defined and proclaimed, yet again, as the historic homeland and nation-state of the Jewish people, declaring that only Jews have the right to self-determination there. Hebrew has been declared as the official language of Israel and Arabic now has a special status; the use of Arabic in state institutions will be regulated by law. The adoption of the law has been met with criticism from across the world and within Israel on grounds that it legalizes forms of discrimination, racism, and segregation. But Prime Minister Benjamin Netanyahu reinforced what Israel is and what it is not in a public statement on March 11, 2019, ahead of the forthcoming elections in April, Israel is "the national state, not of all its citizens, but only of the Jewish people" (Chappell and Estrin 2019: 1).

RELIGION AS INSTITUTION AND DISCOURSE: RELIGION-STATE RELATIONSHIP, LEADERS, AND THE DEMOCRACY FACTOR

The relationship between religion and state in Israel is "Neither separation of religion and state nor total integration" (Liebman and Don-Yehiya 1984: 29). Religious belief systems in Israel, especially that of Haredi and Orthodox Judaism through religious political parties, continue to play a significant role in shaping the identity of Israel as a Jewish state and maintaining and safeguarding the Jewish right to land as given in biblical texts. The Jewish identity of the Israeli state, in terms of it being understood as rooted in biblical times, is visible in Israel's body politic and its institutions through numerous symbols. One example is the name "Knesset" for Israel's legislative body, "it was chosen for its connection to *Haknesset Hagdolah*' (Great Assembly), established in the fifth century BCE upon the return of the Jews from their exile in Babylon" (Mazie 2006: 29). A more explicit and powerful symbolic link is the image of the *Magen David* (Star of David) on Israel's national flag, part of Jewish religious identity, which represents the suffering and hope of Jews worldwide throughout the ages. A further example of the nature of the character of the religion–state relationship is evidenced through the legal status and financial support which the chief rabbinate and religious councils receive directly from the state and *Beth Dins* (Orthodox Jewish Religious Courts) have sole responsibility over matters of personal status and family law. This same legal status and financial support are not given to the other two religions in Israel—Christianity and Islam.

A key issue in Israeli public discourse concerns the compatibility of the traditional Jewish law (*Halakhic*), which is central to the dominant form of Judaism practiced in Israel, with that of democracy.

One dominant view is that traditional *Halakhic* Judaism is anti-democratic because of its theocratic nature, "The Jewish religion is not democratic, just as no religion is democratic in the modern liberal sense of the term" (Neuberger 1997: 19). Certainly, this argument appears plausible when applied to those various expressions of religions that promote total adherence in contemporary life to sacred teachings from centuries past, elements of which may be considered to infringe and violate contemporary approaches to rights and equality. However, over the centuries reform has taken place in Jewish understanding, interpretation, and practice of aspects of sacred teachings for the modern world. This is a key character of Reform and Liberal Judaism. These communities in Israel have little influence in the day-to-day running of the state and its decision making, not just because they are numerically much smaller compared to the Haredi and Orthodox communities, but because they do not have the same level of political representation through political parties. While the dominant views of the Israeli Haredi and Orthodox communities continue to advocate no giving back of any land to Palestinians and Negev Bedouin, and instead to continue the expansion of Jewish settlements in Palestinian territory, the dominant view of the Reform and Liberal communities is the opposite. Perhaps a more nuanced view in the discussion of the compatibility of Judaism and liberal democracy is that there are elements in the religio-cultural legacy of Israel (Novak 2012: 6). This legacy is described as "particularly rich in ideas and ideals which could constitute an ideological value infrastructure for the development of democracy" (Langer 1987: 402). But the question remains about whether traditional Jewish *Halakha*, as adhered to by the Haredi and Orthodox Jewish leadership, is able to actually "come to grips" with modern liberal democracy and concepts of the modern age. A response to this question will be key to the second part of this case study in the next chapter. By looking at the work of two Israeli Jewish organizations, the aim is to show that there are two key aspects present in traditional Jewish teaching which have the potential to relate to particular elements of the democratic model: (1) Human beings are created in the image of God and are therefore entitled to equality, and (2) *Halakha* is based on duties and responsibilities of each human being in terms of seeking justice (Falk 1996: 65).

CONCLUSION

The establishment of Israel in 1948 was fraught with difficulties from the outset because this Jewish homeland was created by taking land of which over half of the territory was populated by Arabs, Bedouin, and Palestinians for centuries. The discussion here of religion as community, an institution in relation to the state, and as a set of teachings and action informs us about the role which religion continues to play in promoting and sustaining the Israeli conflict over land. However, it is important to note that this is due to certain expressions of the Jewish tradition (Haredi and Orthodox) having significant influence on most Israeli governments since 1948. As will be discussed in the second half of this case study in the next chapter, there is within the Jewish legacy the potential to promote a world view that can contribute to resolving the conflict over land in Israel.

REFERENCES

Ben-Gurion, David. (1948). *Declaration of Establishment of the State of Israel*. Viewed from www.cfr.org/israel/declaration-establishment-state-israel/ [Date accessed May 21, 2019].

Bureau of Democracy, Human Rights and Labor (BDHRL). (2011). *2010 International Religious Freedom Report*, US Department of State. Viewed from www.state.gov/j/drl/rls/irf/2010_5/168439.htm [Date accessed February 15, 2019].

Chappell, Bill and Estrin, Daniel. (2019). "Netanyahu Says Israel Is 'Nation-State of the Jewish People and Them Alone", WKSU, Kent State University Radio, Ohio. Viewed from www.wksu.org/post/netanyahu-says-israel-nation-state-jewish-people-and-them-alone#stream/0 [Date accessed March 8, 2019].

Falk, Ze'ev. (1996). "Religious Law and Civil Rights", in Natasha Dudinski (ed.), *Religion and State in Israeli and Palestinian Society,* Conference Proceedings, Jerusalem: IPCRI Publications, 58–66.

Frazer, Owen and Friedli, Richard. (2015). *Approaching Religion in Conflict Transformation: Concepts, Cases and Practical Implications*, Center for Security Studies (CSS), ETH Zurich. Viewed from www.css.ethz.ch/content/dam/ethz/special-interest/gess/cis/center-for-securities-studies/pdfs/Approaching-Religion-In-Conflict-Transformation2.pdf [Date accessed June 17, 2019].

Frazer, Owen and Owen, Mark. (2018). *Religion in Conflict and Peacebuilding: Analysis Guide*, Washington, DC, United States Institute of Peace. Viewed from www.usip.org/sites/default/files/USIP_Religion-in-Conflict-Peacebuilding_Analysis-Guide.pdf [Date accessed June 17, 2019].

Harpviken, K.B. and Roislien, H.E. (2005). *Mapping the Terrain: The Role of Religion in Peace-Making.* Oslo: PRIO.

Israeli Ministry of Foreign Affairs (IMFA). (n.d.). *Israel's War of Independence (1947–1949).* Viewed from www.mfa.gov.il/MFA/AboutIsrael/History/Pages/Israels%20War%20of%20Independence%20-%201947%20-%201949.aspx [Date accessed July 5, 2019].

JPost. Com Staff. (2018). "Jewish Nation State Law", *Jerusalem Post*, July 19, 2018.

Langer, M. (1987). "Democracy, Religion and the Zionist Future of Israel", *Judaism: A Quarterly Journal of Jewish Life and Thought*, 36(4): 400–415.

Marx, Emanuel. (1967). *Bedouin of the Negev.* Manchester: Manchester University Press.

Mazie, Steven V. (2006). *Israel's Higher Law – Religion and Liberal Democracy in the Jewish State.* New York: Lexington Books.

Morris, Benny. (2008). *1948: The First Arab-Israeli War.* Yale: Yale University Press.

Nachman, Ben-Yehuda (2010) *Theocratic Democracy: The Social Construction of Religious and Secular Extremism.* Oxford: Oxford University Press.

Neuberger, Benjamin. (1997). *Religion and Democracy in Israel.* Jerusalem: Ahva Press Ltd.

Novak, David. (2012). "Is Democracy a Jewish Idea?" Extracts from Symposium Discussion, September 20, 2012, *Moment*, September-October. Viewed from www.momentmag.com/symposium-is-democracy-a-jewish-idea/ [Date accessed April 30, 2019].

Rosenbaum, Alan. (2019). "Inscribing the Jewish Future on Masada", *The Jerusalem Post*, June 21, 2019. Viewed from www.jpost.com/Diaspora/Inscribing-the-Jewish-future-on-Masada-593211 [Date accessed July 7, 2019].

Swirski, Shlomo and Hasson, Yael (2006) Invisible Citizens: Israeli Government Policy toward the Negev Bedouin, The Centre for Bedouin Studies and Development Research Unit, Beer Sheva: Ben Gurion University of the Negev Publications.

United Nations Conciliation Commission for Palestine (UNCCP). (1950). *General Progress Report and Supplementary Report of the United Nations Conciliation Commission for Palestine*, Covering the Period from December 11, 1949 to October 23, 1950. (UN General Assembly Official Records, 5th Session, Supplement No. 18, Document A/1367/Rev. 1).

United Nations Office for the Coordination of Humanitarian Affairs (UN OCHA). (2011). "Barrier Update: Special Focus". Viewed from www.ochaopt.org/documents/ocha_opt_barrier_update_july_2 [Date accessed July 6, 2019].

5

CHRISTIAN PERSPECTIVE
RELIGION IN PRE-GENOCIDE
AND GENOCIDE RWANDA

Christine Schliesser

CHRISTIAN CHURCHES: ACCOMPLICES IN GENOCIDE?

When the genocide scorched Rwanda in 1994, killing up to one million people in its wake, it was seen not only as the culmination of a civil war raging since 1990, but of decades of ethnic mass violence. Since Rwanda's independence in 1962, repeated massacres between the Tutsi minority of the country (about 15 percent) and the Hutu majority had left hundreds of thousands of people dead. In the genocide, while most victims were Tutsi, countless moderate Hutu who refused to participate in the bloodbath were murdered as well. Different from previous eruptions of violence, this time the churches no longer functioned as sanctuaries. Instead, they became morgues. More people were killed in churches and parishes than anywhere else. Combined with the fact that over 90 percent of the Rwandan population consider themselves Christians, this begs the question of what role religion—and more concretely: Christianity—played before and during the genocide. Up to this day, the involvement of the churches remains controversial as the questions surrounding a "complicity of the Churches" (Rittner, Roth, and Whitworth 2004) have not yet been fully answered. Complicity in the genocide goes beyond wielding a machete or denouncing refugees. Complicity also involves creating and sustaining the conditions in which the genocide could occur. In order to get a better understanding of the "religious factor" in the Rwandan genocide, I will use the six-dimensional model outlined in Chapter 3 in order to approach religion in this conflict (Frazer and Owen 2018; Frazer and Friedli 2015). Of the six dimensions of religion, four feature prominently in the context of Rwanda, namely: religion as community, as a set of teachings, as discourse, and as an institution.

RELIGION AS COMMUNITY: RELIGIOUS VS. ETHNIC IDENTITIES AND RELATIONSHIPS

Different from other ethno-religious conflicts, for instance, in Northern Nigeria or Sri Lanka where varying religious traditions are a major factor, the genocide in Rwanda took place within one and the same religious community. Christians were killing Christians. Divisions were not even along denominational lines such as in the Northern Ireland conflict between Protestants and Catholics. Rather, people of the same faith traditions, even from within the same local church congregation, murdered each other. The divider aspect of religion as community that encourages thinking in terms of "us" vs. "them" along religious lines therefore does not seem to pertain to the Rwandan situation. Nor does the connecting aspect that rests on the assumption that religious communities create a strong communal identity, transcending other divisive factors such as ethnicity. Instead, it appears that in Rwanda identity was viewed in terms of ethnicity rather than religion. Here, one needs to keep in mind that the terms "Hutu", "Tutsi", and "Twa" (a small minority of ca. 1 percent) are not conventional ethnic descriptions. Rather, they were used to denote professions and/or wealth. Whoever owned more than ten cattle was considered a herdsman or Tutsi. Whoever had less was a Hutu, a farmer. Twa were traditionally potters (Bataringaya 2012: 22). It was only the colonial powers—first Germany, then Belgium after World War I—who cemented these differences into ethnic categories through their strategy of divide-and-rule. Notwithstanding the historical responsibility of Europe for the ethnic-political conflicts in Africa, Rwanda seems to prove that the blood of ethnicity is thicker than the water of baptism. In marked contrast, the small Muslim community in Rwanda was not drawn into the genocide as their shared Muslim identity transcended the Hutu-Tutsi distinction (Prunier 1995: 253).

Yet despite the apparent prominence of ethnicity, the nexus of religion, community and Christian identity is more complex. Religious identity was recreated on a different level as ethnic identities became sacralized into pseudo-religious identities. The most powerful religious player in pre-genocide Rwanda, the Catholic Church, endorsed the state's unjust ethnic policies. Their mission strategy rested largely on ethnicity as they targeted the elite for conversion, first, favoring Tutsi, then Hutu. Ethnicity thus became enmeshed with religion, it became religiously charged and turned into a sacralized ethnic identity, grotesquely illuminated by génocidaires taking daily communion during the genocide to strengthen themselves for their "work".

The work of René Girard on religion and violence helps to illuminate the nexus of religion, communities, identities, and relationships. According to Girard, human relations are based on reciprocity; we live in "mimetic" relationships. The reason for this is desire. Human conflict in turn is therefore not so much about differences, such as in ideology, religion or ethnicity, but about rivalry (Girard 1998: 132). Given humans' inclination for desire and competition and the mimetic nature of our relationships, mimetic rivalry can quickly turn into a spiral of increasing hostility and violence. Small misgivings are retaliated by bigger offenses and so on. Archaic communities, Girard points out, had a sacred built-in braking mechanism in the mimetic spiral.

> When you have that mimetic violence, there comes a point when you forget about the object and you concentrate on your opponent ... and there is a tendency for the system to simplify itself ... until finally everyone polarizes against a single enemy who seems responsible for the whole crisis.
>
> (Girard 1998: 133)

This single enemy is the scapegoat. The escalating violence can be brought only to a halt once the scapegoat is killed, thus mirroring the sacred ritual of the Old Testament scapegoat killed for the sake of the people. In this ritual, the scapegoat becomes both victim and sacrifice.

This quick overview already reveals its pertinence for the Rwandan context. The deliberate creation of fixed ethnic boundaries combined with decades of colonial policies of favor and disfavor had intensified ethnic rivalries, offsetting a spiral of violence with repeated massacres. From this perspective, artificially constructed differences in terms of ethnicity are therefore just the façade for the problem underneath, namely rivalry. Rivalry in Rwanda has many faces, ranging from a feeling of inferiority on the side of the group in disfavor with the colonial powers over an unjust quota system in education to the scarcity of natural resources such as land. In a context of ingrained cultural violence (see below: Religion as a set of teachings: problematic theology) and structural violence by the colonial powers, the step to direct violence is a small one indeed. Once the spiral of mimetic violence had escalated, the system's tendency for self-simplification started showing and the need for a victim-sacrifice arose. Killing the scapegoat—the Tutsi—bestowed a sense of sacralization to both the scapegoat and the killers. While Girard's theory must not be overstretched in the effort to understand the nature of violence in Rwanda, it helps to shed light on certain aspects, such as the role of mimetic relationships and the sacred ritual of killing a scapegoat. Rather than exposing and confronting the underlying rivalry between Hutu and Tutsi and the escalation of violence, the churches supported the existing ethnic divisions. It is "by making ethnic violence understandable and acceptable to the population … [that] Churches helped to make genocide possible" (Longman 2001: 166).

RELIGION AS A SET OF TEACHINGS: PROBLEMATIC THEOLOGY

Approaching religion as a set of teachings in pre-genocide and genocide Rwanda provides another helpful angle for understanding the role of religion in this context. From the Christian message with its core concepts of love and mercy, how could such atrocious acts of hatred spring forth? One line of thought tries to explain this paradox in terms of a superficial faith. From this perspective, the mass conversions to Catholic Christianity following the baptism of Rwanda's King Mutara III Rudahigwa in 1943 were seen as guided mainly by strategic purposes, rather than denoting a genuine transformation of hearts and minds. While this argument might hold a certain validity, it does not take that into account which appears to be at the core of the paradox: theology itself.

The theological teachings disseminated by both the early missionaries and later the institutionalized churches emphasized respect for authorities, not least for the hierarchy of the Church, and obedience to the state. Furthermore, the Christian religion was portrayed as a spiritual, inner affair with no bearing on public life. "Christian identity was socially and politically irrelevant" (Carney 2014: 119). In the aftermath of World Wars I and II, eschatology figured prominently in the churches' teachings. Believers were told to look to their rewards in heaven, rather than being burdened by the life in this world (Munyaneza 2001: 64). This-worldly issues such as poverty, injustice, and violence were not to be concerns of the Christian, but better left to politicians. While obedience to authority is indeed one aspect of the Christian Scripture (such as in Romans 13), the teachings of the churches neglected other crucial aspects such as active love for the neighbor (as illustrated by the Parable of the Good Samaritan in Luke 10:25–37) that extends even to one's enemy (Matthew 5:44).

Rwandan converts hardly learned about important Christian concepts such as responsibility, freedom, and the prophetic witness of speaking truth to power. Even as massacres of Tutsi were taking place throughout the country during the Civil War 1990–1993, the church leaders mostly failed to name or condemn them. For instance, in their Easter message of March 1991, the Catholic bishops preached on the love of enemies, yet failed to address the massacre of Tutsi at Ruhengeri in the previous month. And even when the massacres were mentioned, blame was allocated to Hutu or Tutsi rather than the government. Chained to a highly dubious theological justification of loyalty to ecclesiastical hierarchy and state power, Christian-based social justice remained a thin concept, even as younger priests tried to carry some of the atmosphere of change of the Second Vatican Council into the Rwandan context. Though there were notable exceptions, one needs to conclude that by failing to speak out against ethnicity-based injustices—ranging from discrimination over exclusion to murder—and by failing to condemn state instigated hatred, the churches gave the impression that they condoned the expanding violence against the Tutsi as in line with

Christian belief. "The churches, thus, not only failed to provide an obstacle along the path towards genocide but actually helped to create a moral climate where genocide was possible" (Longman 2010: 162f.).

RELIGION AS DISCOURSE: LANGUAGE, CULTURAL MYTHS, AND *WELTANSCHAUUNG*

Religion as discourse is yet another fruitful lens to employ. Approaching religion through discourse means, first of all, taking a closer look at language. Drawing on pseudo-theological notions of duty and loyalty to authorities, Christian language was often instrumentalized for political purposes. For example, after the Tutsi RPF (Rwanda Patriotic Front) Army had invaded Rwanda from the North in 1990, sparking the civil war that culminated in the 1994 genocide, the religious language of Christian unity and duty was invoked to appeal for national unity and the obligation to serve one's country. On October 12, 1990, Vincent Nsengiyumva, Archbishop of Kigali and member of the central committee of the ruling party until 1990, reminded Catholics of their "duty of protecting the country against all peril and against all menace, from wherever it comes—from the interior or the exterior" (cited in Carney 2014: 197). Jean-Pierre Karegeye thus rightly points to the "strong interaction in political and religious speeches [that] facilitated the way to genocide" (Karegeye 2011: 97).

Yet religion as discourse goes beyond language as a system for communication and extends to a cultural and linguistic framework that molds the entire life. For a better understanding of how mentalities on religion and violence developed in the context of Rwanda, we need to go back to pre-colonial times. Long before the arrival of Christianity at the turn of the 20th century, religion was already an integral part of Rwandan life. The spiritual world, inhabited by a heavenly Being called Imana and other spirits, was believed to have a direct influence on the living. Participation in different cults, such as that of Lyangombe or Nyabingi, offered access to spiritual powers. Like other parts of Rwandan oral history, these cults were vibrant with violent images, stories, and initiation rites. Forming the cultural and linguistic background, "the stories told and learnt by heart, orally and transmitted, were full of violent images ... and the banalization of violence and death" (Munyaneza 2001: 58). Christianity failed to address this cultural heritage of violence. Not only did Christianity not challenge it, but contributed to reinforcing latent violence, for instance, by using Kinyarwanda words associated with violence in the translation of the Bible and hymns. God and Jesus Christ, for example, are called *umutabazi* (savior/liberator). In Rwandan oral history and cultural myths, however, this term is inseparably connected to the glorification of violence as it refers to quasi-mythical heroes who were sacrificed for their people.

Rwandan traditional *Weltanschauung* was further characterized by the belief in predetermination and fatalism. The experience of misfortune or violence was met with resignation as the expression of Imana's will or as the result of angry spirits one had failed to pacify. This thinking aligned itself only too easily with Christian ideas of predetermination. At times, biblical narratives were employed to justify ethnic differences. "Especially the Book of Genesis was used to prove that *Abatutsi* pastoralists were like Abel, and *Abahutu* like Cain who was agriculturist and who fell in disgrace and therefore was cursed" (Munyaneza 2001: 64). Instead of addressing and critically examining the violence latent in Rwandan history and cultural myths, the churches ignored or worse, contributed to cultural violence. This failure on the side of the churches helped to sustain conditions in which violence and injustice could be understood as preordained and therefore inevitable, making the struggle against it seem pointless.

RELIGION AS AN INSTITUTION: CHURCH-STATE RELATIONS, THE CONSTRUCTION OF HEGEMONY, AND POWER STRUGGLES

In order to better understand the role of religion in creating the conditions for genocide to occur, we also need to look at religion as an institution. Here, the following three aspects come into view: a church-state relationship that lacked critical distance, the construction of hegemony, and power struggles within the Church. Given the prominence of the Catholic Church in pre-genocide Rwanda, we will be looking at this church in particular. In 1900, the so-called White Fathers, a French Catholic Missionary Order, were the first

Christian missionaries entering Rwanda. The White Fathers aimed to convert the elites first, hoping that the masses would follow. Since the native king, Yuhi V Musinga, was a Tutsi, the missionaries focused on the Tutsi. When after World War I Belgium succeeded Germany as the colonial power, the new colonial rulers relied on the White Fathers for their cultural experience as they implemented a policy favoring Tutsi over Hutu. Tensions between the two groups intensified when the Belgian authorities issued identity cards that cemented ethnic affiliation, making race the central identity marker. Throughout their rule, colonial authorities collaborated closely with the Catholic Church. When King Musinga resisted conversion, his son Mutara III Rudahigwa, a devout Catholic, was implemented as his successor. "There was a perfect relationship between Church and State" (Van't Spijker 1997: 241).

Increasingly, it became apparent that church affiliation was a way to achieve political power and the masses followed when their king was baptized in 1943. Even after Rwanda's independence in 1962, the Catholic Church continued to grow, until 65 percent of the population were members of the Catholic Church. Examples like the already mentioned Vincent Nsengiyumva, who was both Archbishop of Kigali and a member of the central committee of the ruling party until the Vatican forced him to resign from all political posts, illustrate the close ties between the state and the Church. While too much distance between Church and state can result in a church that is disengaged and disinterested in worldly affairs, too little distance can result in a lack of critical prophetic witness on the side of the church. The latter was clearly the case in Rwanda. Even during the civil war and genocide, official Church statements would shy away from criticizing the government openly, thus giving the impression of implicit support of the government's actions.

Church affiliation was not only seen as an entrance into the sphere of political power but linked to power and opportunity in general. Oftentimes, the Church was the main community supplier of jobs, education, health care, and other resources. Being educated and possibly sponsored in a church school was often the only chance of escaping the spiral of poverty. The hierarchy within the Church was thus mirrored in society through the construction of hegemony. Much power was concentrated in the hands of few deciding who would get hired and fired and who would receive financial or practical aid. Even when the churches' policy changed from privileging Tutsi to favoring Hutu after 1959, the underlying structures remained in place. With the Church being the main source of practical help and opportunities, dependents had little choice but to consent to its policies. This was a problem not only in the Catholic Church, but also in Protestant denominations that had sprung up since 1907. Timothy Longman describes the construction of hegemony in view of the Presbyterian Church.

> While supporting the dominant class position of a limited elite and providing little real opportunity for advancement to the majority of people in the parish, a patrimonial system within the church created dependency in the subordinate classes that limited their ability to challenge the system.
>
> (Longman 2010: 221)

Antonio Gramsci's analysis of power is helpful here, as he describes the emergence of a "false consciousness" by the powerless who seem to have internalized the oppressive ideology. Yet next to a "false consciousness" (Gramsci 1971: 12), it is also the dire necessity of having no practical alternatives that led to people's acceptance of the status quo.

At the same time, reform movements from within the churches increasingly questioned the patrimonial system of power, the lack of transparency, and susceptibility to corruption. New ideas from liberation theology challenged especially the Catholic Church to become progressive agents of social change on behalf of the poor. In the 1980s and early 1990s, massive power struggles evolved within the Church as conservative and progressive strands fought for influence. Conservative parts within the Church saw the new democratic and social movements as threats to their own power. They thus perceived of the genocide as conducive to preserving the status quo. "Many church leaders were ultimately sympathetic to the genocide because it could help to bolster their power and preserve their hold on office against this movement for reform" (Longman 2001: 175).

CHRISTIAN CHURCHES IN RWANDA: COLLABORATORS IN VIOLENCE, WITNESSES FOR PEACE

By approaching religion as community, as set of teachings, as discourse, and as an institution, we have gained a better understanding of the role of religion in creating and maintaining the conditions in which ultimately the Rwandan genocide could take place. Yet to portray all Christian churches per se as genocide collaborators would be a misrepresentation. While our discussion has already revealed a multifaceted picture, it becomes even more complex when we take the numerous initiatives for peace and reconciliation by individuals and church communities before the genocide into account. As the focus of this chapter is on the conflictive side of religion rather than its peacebuilding capacities, a few examples must suffice here (cf. Schliesser 2018). One prominent effort for de-escalation and peace was the creation of the so-called Contact Committee in the middle of the civil war, in 1991, by ten Protestant and Catholic Church leaders. It was meant to provide a platform for mediation between the different political parties, especially between the government and the RPF, encouraging democratization and political reconciliation (Gatwa 2005: 206–208). While it could ultimately not prevent the genocide, it helped facilitate the transition to a multiparty system. Still on the eve of the genocide, on January 1, 1994, the Contact Committee organized a peace march for all Christians across denominations. Thousands of Christians marched and prayed for peace in Rwanda's capital, Kigali, and other cities throughout the country.

Next to Church initiatives, countless individuals withstood the violence, at times paying for their courage with their lives. When ethnic violence was rampant in December 1991, Thaddée Nsengiyumva, bishop of Kabgayi and President of the Rwandan Episcopal conference, issued a pastoral letter "*Convertissons-nous pour vivre ensemble dans la paix*" ("Let us convert to live together in peace") (Nsengiyumva 1991). In this pastoral letter, Nsengiyumva admonished his church to take responsibility for its part in creating and sustaining ethnic divisions and called for a renewal within the Church. During the genocide, Nsengiyumva repeatedly issued public calls for the killings to stop as he assisted the International

Committee of the Red Cross (ICRC) in caring for war displaced people in his bishopric. He was murdered on June 5, 1994.

A flat description, therefore, of all Christians or all churches as implicated in the genocide does not do justice to the numerous individual and Church-led efforts at peace and reconciliation. Despite their courage, however, these initiatives were not representative of the overall attitudes on the side of the churches. For the most part, instead of openly criticizing ethnic violence, church leaders continued to call for support of the government. "In distancing itself from the Rwandan genocidal regime, the church would have had the chance to cut off the moral support to political violence" (Karegeye 2011: 100). Instead, the churches remained silent.

REFERENCES

Bataringaya, Pascal. (2012). *Versöhnung nach dem Genozid. Impulse der Friedensethik Dietrich Bonhoeffers für Kirche und Gesellschaft in Ruanda.* Kamen: Spenner.

Carney, James J. (2014). *Rwanda Before the Genocide. Catholic Politics and Ethnic Discourse in the Late Colonial Era.* New York: Oxford University Press.

Frazer, Owen and Friedli, Richard. (2015). *Approaching Religion in Conflict Transformation: Concepts, Cases and Practical Implications,* Center for Security Studies (CSS), ETH Zurich. Viewed from www.css.ethz.ch/content/dam/ethz/special-interest/gess/cis/center-for-securities-studies/pdfs/Approaching-Religion-In-Conflict-Transformation2.pdf [Date accessed November 1, 2019].

Frazer, Owen and Owen, Mark. (2018). *Religion in Conflict and Peacebuilding: Analysis Guide.* Washington, DC, United States Institute of Peace. Viewed from www.usip.org/sites/default/files/USIP_Religion-in-Conflict-Peacebuilding_Analysis-Guide.pdf [Date accessed November 1, 2019].

Gatwa, Tharcisse. (2005). *The Churches and Ethnic Ideology in the Rwandan Crises 1900–1994.* Milton Keynes: Regnum Books International.

Girard, René. (1998). "Victims, Violence and Christianity", *The Month,* 4(31): 129–135.

Gramsci, Antonio. (1971). *Selections from the Prison Notebooks.* New York: International Publishers.

Karegeye, Jean-Pierre. (2011). "Religion, Politics, and Genocide in Rwanda", in Andrea Bieler, Bingel, Christian, and Gutmann, Hans-Martin (eds.), *After Violence: Religion, Trauma and Reconciliation.* Leipzig: Evangelische Verlagsanstalt, 82–102.

Longman, Timothy. (2001). "Church Politics and the Genocide in Rwanda", *Journal of Religion in Africa,* 31: 163–86.

Longman, Timothy. (2010). *Christianity and Genocide in Rwanda*. New York: Cambridge University Press.

Munyaneza, Malachie. (2001). "Violence as Institution in African Religious Experience: A Case Study of Rwanda", *Contagion: Journal of Violence, Mimesis, and Culture*, 8: 39–68.

Nsengiyumva, Thaddée. (1991). *Convertissons-Nous Pour Vivre Ensemble Dans La Paix*. Gitarama: Diocése de Kabgayi.

Prunier, Gérard. (1995). *The Rwanda Crisis: History of a Genocide*. New York: Columbia University Press.

Rittner, Carol, Roth, John K., and Whitworth, Wendy (eds.). (2004). *Genocide in Rwanda. Complicity of the Churches?* St. Paul, Minnesota: Paragon House.

Schliesser, Christine. (2018). "From 'A Theology of Genocide' to a 'Theology of Reconciliation'? On the Role of Christian Churches in the Nexus of Religion and Genocide in Rwanda", *Religions. Special Issue Religion and Genocide*, 9(34): 1–14. doi:10.3390/rel9020034

Van't Spijker, Gerard. (1997). "The Churches and the Genocide in Rwanda", *Exchange*, 26: 233–255.

6

ISLAMIC PERSPECTIVE
RELIGION IN PAKISTAN'S INTERNAL CONFLICTS

S. Ayse Kadayifci-Orellana

INTRODUCTION

Pakistan became the epicenter of extremist violence and the war against it following the attacks of September 11, 2001, when 19 militants hijacked four planes and attacked targets in the United States (US), killing almost 3,000 people and injuring many more. Al-Qaeda, led by Osama bin Laden, claimed the attacks in the name of Islam. In response, the US and its allies, including Pakistan, initiated a military offensive against al-Qaeda, and demanded the Taliban government of Afghanistan hand bin Laden over to the US. The Taliban government had, however, given refuge to al-Qaeda prior to the attacks and refused to surrender bin Laden.

Taliban soldiers and leaders in Afghanistan were originally recruited from refugee camps in Pakistan at a young age and were sent to Deobandi madrasas, where they were indoctrinated with the idea of jihad (Malik 2008; Rahman 2008; Looney 2003; Ali 2009). These madrasas and mosques continued to spread a radical interpretation of jihad that targeted local and international "enemies" and contributed to sectarian violence. Although using religion to justify violence is neither unique to Islam nor a recent phenomenon, Islam, which is derived from the word *slm* (peace), and jihad (struggle), has come to be associated with violence and terrorism. As a result, religion and politics in Pakistan have gained international attention and Pakistan's madrasa system of Islamic education has come under intense scrutiny (International Crisis Group (ICG) 2002, 2003).

This case study explores the role religion played in the rise of extremist violence in Pakistan. The discussion will first explore how religion as community contributed to the construction of Pakistani identity during and after its establishment as a nation-state in 1947. It will then explain how religion as a set of teachings was influential in the emergence of a particular interpretation of Islamic understanding of jihad in madrasas and mosques. Finally, it will investigate how religion as a discourse has caused tensions amongst various interpretations of jihad and how groups such as the Taliban and al-Qaeda have tried to justify their interpretation of the term.

PAKISTAN AND VIOLENCE IN THE NAME OF ISLAM

The Islamic Republic of Pakistan was founded on August 14, 1947, when the country gained independence from the British Commonwealth. At the time of its establishment, it consisted of West Pakistan and East Pakistan. East Pakistan seceded to establish Bangladesh in 1971 after a civil war. Pakistan continued to have territorial conflicts on the Afghan–Pakistan border and in the disputed Kashmir region. Today, Pakistan is the sixth most populous country in the world with a dynamic and emerging economy (World Bank 2019). As the only Muslim-majority country with nuclear weapons it is also considered a regional power.

Since its emergence, Pakistan has had a complicated relationship with Islam, which has been used as a source of legitimacy by both governments and militant groups. There are a number of different militant organizations operating in Pakistan with al-Qaeda being the most recognized one. The origins of al-Qaeda date back to the Afghan–Soviet war (1979–1989) when global Muslim fighters known as *Mujahedeen*—supported by the CIA, the Kingdom of Saudi Arabia, Egypt, and the Pakistani Intelligence Agency—initiated an insurgency to fight the Soviet invasion. During this period, many al-Qaeda leaders and fighters received training in madrasas in Pakistan and as a result of their collaboration in the

Afghan war developed close bonds with other Pakistani extremist groups, particularly the Taliban.

"Taliban", which means "students" in Pashto, is the main umbrella group for the Afghan insurgency as well as the name of a number of different radical Deobandi Sunni groups in Pakistan. The Taliban emerged following the Afghan war in the mid-1990s. In Pakistan, different groups operating under the name Taliban came together in 2007 to form a political coalition of militias called Tehrik-i-Taliban (TTP). While they are distinct groups with a different history and leadership, Afghani and Pakistani Taliban often fight alongside each other. Each control different areas and have different agendas and political objectives but are directly supported by al-Qaeda and share a similar ideology. Other extremist groups in Pakistan include Hizb-ul-Mujahideen, Jaish-e-Mohammed (JeM), and Lashkar-e-Taiba (LeT), which focus mainly on jihad in Kashmir, and anti-Shiite groups such as Laskhar-Jhangvi and Sipah-e-Sahaba Pakistan, which aim to establish Pakistan as a mainly Deobandi-Sunni state.

While each of these organizations has different goals and focus, and do not adhere to the same Sunni interpretative tradition, they all seek their legitimacy within an Islamic framework, and want to enforce Sharia (Islamic Law). What differs is their geographical focus, targets, and military tactics. For example, al-Qaeda and its affiliates are responsible for atrocities around the world including the 1988 bombings of the US embassies in Tanzania and Kenya, the 2003 and 2005 bombings in Madrid and London, and others. Additionally, they target governments of Muslim-majority countries because they consider them illegitimate for being corrupt, impotent, and in collaboration with Western governments. Groups like LeT target India in Kashmir (Afzal 2018: 8). The government of Pakistan treats each of these groups differently: Pakistan is engaged in military operations against TTP but continues to provide sanctuary to Afghan Taliban and groups that fight against Indian forces in Kashmir (Afzal 2018: 6).

RELIGION AS COMMUNITY: ISLAM AND PAKISTANI IDENTITY

The rise of militant Islam in Pakistan cannot be understood without exploring the role religion played in the construction of Pakistani identity. Religion has been an important source of identity and a tool for political legitimacy in Pakistan since its foundation in 1947, although the founders of Pakistan, such as Mohammed Ali Jinnah, conceived of a secular, pluralistic state, and not a theocratic one. Religious traditions often play an important role in defining group identity, defining who belongs to the group and who does not, and legitimating particular national objectives. Islam, similar to other religious traditions, holds reservoirs of meaning that shape Muslim identities and incorporate values, texts, and symbols that give expression to collective needs and desires. Islam, both as a religion and a cultural framework, informs the identities of Muslims as individuals and as Muslim communities (*ummah*), and it offers a set of vocabulary and meanings that legitimize various socio-political projects. Islam provides believers with a moral framework that guides their actions and plays a profound role in the molding of social structures and the justification of the social and political order. Muslim leaders often resort to the inimitable power of religion to mobilize the population towards their goals, especially at times of conflict and war. Paradoxically, religion is often used as a legitimizing force both for governments and those who oppose them.

In Pakistan, both political leaders and leaders of militant Islamic groups have sought legitimacy for their policies by framing them within an Islamic framework. The emotional resonance that extremists manage to generate in their Pakistani audiences has roots in the narratives that were developed and deployed in the establishment of Pakistan and in subsequent historical events (Khan 2013: 2). "Religion has always been described as the single most important basis of Muslim nationhood, and Islam was employed as a means of fostering group identity to mobilize the masses in the pre-independence period" (Islam 1981: 56).

Islam as an integrative force was critical in defining Pakistani national identity (Saqib 1983: 194) and was successfully utilized to mobilize mass support for Pakistan during its establishment (Islam 1981: 57). The idea of Pakistani nationhood separate from India was based on the perceived ethnic religious differences between Hindu and Muslim communities. For Muhammed Ali Jinnah, founder and first governor of Pakistan, being a Muslim in India was a "matter of identity, a form of ethno-cultural distinction"; therefore, Muslims in

India were a distinct nation from Hindus (Afzal 2018: 34). Muslim League leaders, such as Jinnah, needed a framework for legitimacy to build the identity of a new state, and often invoked the idea that Islam and Muslims in India were in danger and used Muslim identity as a glue to hold together different Muslims' ethnicities in Pakistan. Muslims in India consisted of various ethnic groups and spoke different languages. Poet and philosopher Allama Iqbal (1875–1938), often credited with being the father of Pakistani Islamic identity (Islam 1981: 55), believed that Islamic identity could bring these different ethnic and linguistic groups together as an *ummah* (the Muslim community), connect them with the wider Muslim world, and preserve the Islamic way of life.

Over the course of its history, multiple leaders have resorted to Islam to legitimize their policies and seek public support. Still, the rise of General Zia ul-Haq to power in 1977 was a turning point in the Islamization of Pakistan, especially as he started his intensive Islamization policies. General Haq, a practicing Muslim himself, used Islam to legitimize his domestic power and to undermine opposition. He took both a legal and cultural attitude to Islamicize the country by first enforcing Islamic laws and establishing Sharia courts and then by using madrasas and other Islamic institutions to increase support. With his education policy in 1979, he facilitated the integration of madrasas into the Pakistani education system. This policy resulted in "Islamic" elements being added to the curricula at all educational levels. The basic aim of this policy was to create a new generation of Muslims imbued with Islam.

War against the Soviets in the 1980s provided a new opportunity for Pakistan's Islamization. While the military regime used Islam internally to gain political legitimacy, the concept of jihad was used externally to arouse religious sentiments and mobilize guerilla bands of *mujahideen* (fighters) against the Soviets in Afghanistan (Shah 2012: 310).

> The Pakistani establishment, including its armed forces and intelligence agencies, strongly supported conservative Sunni radicals and the Taliban movement to gain putative strategic depth through a subordinated Afghanistan and by preempting the formation of a hostile Indian–Afghanistan consortium.
>
> (Simon and Stevenson 2009: 47)

When the war in Afghanistan ended, Kashmir became the new arena of jihad for Islamic militants, supported by the Pakistani Government (Lamb and Mufti 2012: 18).

Taliban and al-Qaeda also frame their objectives and strategies within the Islamic framework to justify them and use Islamic identity to mobilize followers. Brian Fisherman and Assaf Moghadam (2010: 6) argue that the ideology of the global jihadi movement aims to make Muslims aware that Islam is in a state of decline relative to its past glory, and identify the reasons for this decline in the attacks by anti-Islamic Crusaders, Zionists, and apostates. In order to respond to this threat, this ideology aims to create a new Muslim identity by offering them membership of the globalized community of believers and to present jihad as program of action (Fishman and Moghdam 2016). This form of Muslim identity is closely tied to practicing a particular interpretation of Islamic law and lifestyle that is rooted in the Sunni Wahhabi tradition. To mobilize support, these groups invoke the concept of *ummah* to create solidarity and unity amongst Muslims and to urge them to take responsibility for issues involving Muslims globally. An Islamic framework is used to define the contours of relationships between Muslims and non-Muslims. Those who do not follow this interpretation are considered to be living in ignorance and, therefore, are not true Muslims. For example, Zawahiri, in his articulation of Muslim identity, points out that those not residing in Islamic land and not living according to Wahhabi interpretation and application of Sharia Law, including fellow Muslims, are regarded as apostate infidels who must be purged (Rogan 2010: 409). Also, in his treatise "The Foundations of Loyalty and Enmity in Islam", he describes friends and enemies of Muslims, and urges Muslims to not to take "infidels" as friends or allies (Ibrahim 2007). Using the *takfiri* doctrine (the process of ex-communicating Muslims for not being pious enough) these groups argue that Pakistani Government's collaboration with the US makes them justifiable targets for jihad (Lamb and Mufti 2012: 19–20).

RELIGION AS A SET OF TEACHINGS: MADRASAS AND JIHAD

Religion as a set of ideas refers to a shared set of teachings, doctrines, norms, values, and narratives that provide a framework for understanding and acting in the world. These religious ideas and teachings can be used to support peace and tolerance or justify violence and conflict. An ideology and doctrine of jihad that justified attacks on local and international enemies were often promoted at some of the Deobandi madrasas in Pakistan based on their interpretation of religious verses, teachings, and stories. Madrasas, or Islamic schools, have come under scrutiny following the 9/11 attacks because many of the Taliban soldiers and leaders in Afghanistan, including Mullah Omar (who was recognized as the Commander of the Faithful or the Supreme Leader by Taliban), were originally recruited from refugee camps in Pakistan at a young age and were sent to madrasas, where they were indoctrinated with the idea of jihad (Malik 2008). Rashid (2000: 4) states that, "Taliban interpretation of sharia was influenced by extremist Deobandi teachings in Pakistan, a perversion of Pashtunwali [the traditional Pashtun code of conduct], and its harsh enforcement all over Afghanistan". The Taliban's ideology was influenced by Deobandi teachings in Pakistan (Lamb and Mufti 2013: 23). Consequently, Deobandi madrasas in Pakistan came to be associated with fundamentalist institutions that breed Islamic terrorists.

Madrasas have been a major source of religious and scientific learning throughout much of Islamic history. Since the emergence of Islam, madrasas have been part of the Islamic education system. Not all madrasas are pro-violence or preach aggression; however, in Pakistan, prior to British colonization, madrasas were unstructured and served the educational needs of both Muslims and non-Muslims (Zaman 1999). Deobandi religious leaders institutionalized the madrasa system as a reaction to British colonization and imposition of the British education system. During this era, the main purpose of madrasas was to promote Islam and Islamic ethics, while preserving knowledge about the Quran and the traditions of the Prophet. Madrasas became an important tool for Islamization during General Zia's presidency. In order to secure his legitimacy and undermine his mainly secular political opposition, Zia required the support of religious seminaries. His 1979 education policy established a Committee for Dini Madaris to transform the madrasas into an integral part of the Pakistani educational system, and called for 5,000 madrasas to be built (ICG 2002: 11).

Today, many of these institutions are a part of the normal life in Pakistan, and play a key role within the society by educating students from poorer areas in particular. There are five distinct schools of thought within the madrasas in Pakistan today: Wahhabi, Deobandi, Barelvi, Jamat-i-Islami, and Jafria-Shia. In addition to providing Islamic education, madrasas also serve other functions in Pakistani society such as providing shelter, food, and safety for many rural immigrants into urban areas, especially to those poor families who cannot afford to care for their children. These madrasas provide, for the most part, free Islamic education and teach impoverished populations how to read and write (Moosa 2015). They also house thousands of poor people who otherwise lack access to formal education and the fulfillment of basic needs. Thus, the most vulnerable, economically depressed, and impressionable youth of Pakistan end up in the madrasas. Because the very limited education they receive leaves them without any real chance of taking part in the socio-economic growth of their country, many of these young people see their best option as returning to the madrasa as a teacher or joining various groups dissatisfied with their own government or the West, which they view as anti-Islamic.

Texts supporting offensive jihad were not part of the traditional madrasa curriculum, but were developed and included in the madrasa education during the war in Afghanistan, when madrasas started to play an important role in providing the ideological basis of war against the Soviets. Two types of madrasas were particularly active. The first included those madrasas such as Jamaat-e Islami's (JI) *Rabita madrasas*, created specifically to produce jihadi literature to mobilize public opinion and recruit and train military forces (ICG 2002: 11). The second group of madrasas included independent madrasas such as the Jamiat-e Ulama Islam (JUI), which opposed Zia politically but partnered with him during the Afghan war (ICG 2002: 11). These madrasas were supported by the Pakistani military, US, and Arab countries financially, as well as by publishing textbooks in local languages. After the end of the war in Afghanistan these Deobandi madrasas and mosques continued to spread a radical interpretation of jihad that targeted local and international "enemies" and contributed to sectarian violence as well as attacks on the West.

RELIGION AS DISCOURSE: CONTESTED INTERPRETATIONS OF JIHAD

Radicalization of Islamist groups in Pakistan goes back to the early 20th century when Maududi, the founder of Jamaat-e-Islami (JI), articulated his offensive jihad doctrine and elevated it above all other interpretations of jihad within the broader Islamic discourse. Islam as a discourse refers here to the body of thought and writing that is united by having a common object of study, a common methodology used by Islamic scholars, and a set of common terms and ideas it incorporates which is linguistically and culturally specific. It is possible for all Muslims who have been socialized under its authority to speak and act together. Within this discourse, there are different interpretations or narratives. Islamic narratives of jihad are all based on the Islamic discourse rooted in the Quranic verses, sunna, and the hadith. These texts are often filled with ambiguities, contradicting statements, and are written down in a distant time, usually in a language that is different from the ones used by the current communities and must go through human interpretation. Islamic doctrine of jihad is no different, and there are a variety of different interpretations when jihad is permissible and how it should be conducted.

The Arabic word "jihad" literally means "striving" or "struggle", rather than war, as the Quranic verse "strive in the cause of God" (Q22:78) indicates. More specifically, jihad is often understood as a struggle for the cause of God by means of speech, property, wealth, or life. Historically, Muslim scholars differentiated jihad according to its direction (inner and outer) and method (violent and non-violent) (Kadayifci-Orellana, Abu-Nimer, and Mohamed-Saleem 2013). The inner jihad is fought within the individual whereas the outer jihad is seen as a struggle to eliminate evil within the *ummah*. It refers to efforts an individual must make towards self-improvement and self-purification, as well as to the duty of Muslims, both at the individual and collective level, to struggle against all forms of evil, corruption, injustice, tyranny, and oppression. The term "jihad" also refers to use of force to repel an enemy and to fight against injustice and oppression. Scholars of Islamic jurisprudence and law have usually been more concerned with the military form of jihad, as this requires more jurisprudential elaboration and legal regulation (*fiqh*), and Islamic law that deals with war and peace are often included under the title of jihad. In the modern era (19th and 20th centuries), jihad acquired a new momentum and initially took the form of resistance to Western invasion of Islamic lands. Challenged by colonialism, modernization, and globalization, many Islamic thinkers blamed the decline of Muslim power on a deviation from the *right path of Islam* and called for the reinstitution of Islamic rule. Within this context all kinds of resistance movements and leaders adopted jihad as an ideological framework, and as a political rhetoric to justify their policies and conduct.

Multiple interpretations of jihad are a result of the dynamic interaction between the religious texts and changing contextual factors, such as social, political, and cultural contexts, as well as particular historical events. The way religious texts are understood and acted upon during a violent conflict always involves a tension between the fixed text, the word of God, and the particular context of interpretation. However, when leaders use a religious narrative they tend to take them out of a specific context and treat them as if they are fixed, identical, and self-sufficient origins of meaning. They present their interpretation of the religious texts, myths, and symbols as the ultimate truth applicable, regardless of time and place.

There are a variety of possible reasons as to why people choose one interpretation over another. Some of these explanations are related to cognitive and emotional needs that may be met by particular religious imagery, symbolism, and text. Social motivations and personal experiences also play a critical role in determining affiliations with a group that espouses a certain interpretation of religious texts. According to Gopin (2000: 11), the way sacred texts are used to foster peace or promote violence and destruction

> seems to depend on the complex ways in which the psychological and sociological circumstances and the economic and cultural constructs of a particular group interact with the ceaseless human drive to hermeneutically develop religious meaning systems, texts, rituals, symbols, and laws.

Deep fears and concerns also play a significant role in the way religious texts are understood and interpreted, especially at times of war. In return, religious values and texts shape the way individuals view their conflict, perceive their enemies, and make sense of their suffering and ways to address them.

Al-Qaeda and Taliban argue that the current global economic-political system only breeds oppression, injustice, and exploitation; therefore, it must be removed and replaced by God's governance. Framing their jihad as a retaliation to injustice, oppression, and aggression of the West and its secular allies in the Muslim world, they invoke military jihad as an obligation of every Muslim. In order to increase popular support, they explain that jihad today is a global revolutionary struggle, which must be fought by any means, including violence, political action, and propaganda against the Western powers as well as secular Muslim regimes. In this, "jihad" attacks against civilian targets are necessary evils to bring God's rule to earth (Ibrahim 2007).

Islamic symbols, language, imagery, as well as Islamic texts are used to spread this ideology through mosques, madrasas, videos, and propaganda on social media. Most Deobandi literature traces the history of how Muslims have repeatedly been subjugated by the "Zionist occupation of Palestine, Indian occupation of Kashmir, Russian occupation of Chechnya, and subjugation of Muslim States in the Philippines" (Haqqani 2005: 22). Framing the conflict within a religious framework, these extremist groups aim to provide an ideology which conceives of the world in a coherent and manageable way, and to offer explanations for worldly events, including human suffering, and the response to it. Using Quranic verses such as "You are obligated to fight even though it is something you do not like" (Q2:216) as well as religious imagery and vocabulary, they legitimize their interpretation of jihad, and construct negative enemy images such as "the Crusaders" linking current conflict to historical ones. With the aid of religious imagery and vocabulary, with which the population is familiar, they provide a cosmology, history, and eschatology of the war and simplify the world into good and evil. They link the past, present, and future in the minds of their followers and invoke emotions such as heroism and vengeance.

CONCLUSION

This chapter showed that the religion of Islam has been instrumentalized to legitimize political objectives both by militant groups and by the government in Pakistan. Islam as a discourse has been utilized to craft the ideology of these groups and this ideology was spread via madrasas, mosques, and other media, using Islamic symbols and texts. However, as it will be shown in the second part of this case study, various Muslim groups and organizations are resorting to the Islamic principles of peace, tolerance, and justice to respond to extremist violence and to build sustainable peace in Pakistan.

REFERENCES

Afzal, Madiha. (2018). *Pakistan Under Siege Extremism, Society, and the State.* Washington, DC: Brookings Institution Press.

Ali, Saleem H. (2009). *Islam and Education: Conflict and Conformity in Pakistan's Madrassahs.* Karachi: Oxford University Press.

Fishman, Brian and Assaf, Moghadam. (2010). *Self-Inflicted Wounds: Debates and Divisions in Al Qaeda's Periphery.* West Point, NY: Combatting Terrorism Center.

Gopin, Marc. (2000). *Between Eden and Armageddon: The Future of World Religions, Violence, and Peacemaking.* Oxford: Oxford University Press.

Haqqani, Hussain. (2005). *Pakistan: Between Mosque and Military.* Washington, DC: Carnegie Endowment for International Peace.

Ibrahim, Raymond. (2007). *The Al Qaeda Reader.* New York: Doubleday.

International Crisis Group. (July 29, 2002). *Pakistan: Madrasas, Extremism and the Militarism.* ICG Asia Report No. 36. [Online]. Viewed from www. crisisgroup.org/asia/south-asia/pakistan/pakistan-madrasas-extremism-and-military [Date accessed June 10, 2019].

International Crisis Group. (March 20, 2003). *Pakistan: The Mullahs and the Military ICG.* Asia Report No. 49. Islamabad/ Brussels. [Online]. Viewed from www.crisisgroup.org/asia/south-asia/pakistan/pakistan-mullahs-and-military [Date accessed June 10, 2019].

Islam, Nasir. (1981). "Islam and National Identity: The Case of Pakistan and Bangladesh", *International Journal of Middle East Studies,* 13(1): 55–72. doi.org/10.1017/S0020743800055070

Kadayifci-Orellana, S. Ayse, Abu-Nimer, Mohammed, and Mohamed-Saleem, Amjad. (2013). "Understanding an Islamic Framework for Peacebuilding". Working Paper Series No. 2013-02. Islamic Relief: London.

Khan, Amil. (March 2013). "Pakistan and the Narratives of Extremism", Special Report 327 USIP. [Online]. Viewed from www.humanitarianlibrary.org/sites/default/files/2014/02/SR327-Pakistan-and-the-Narratives-of-Extremism.pdf [Date accessed October 29, 2019].

Lamb, Robert, D. and Mariam, Mufti. (2012). "Religion and Militancy in Pakistan and Afghanistan: A Literature Review", *Center for Strategic and*

International Studies Report. [Online]. Viewed from https://csis-prod. s3.amazonaws.com/s3fs-public/legacy_files/files/publication/120628_ Mufti_ReligionMilitancy_Web.pdf [Date accessed October 10, 2019].

Looney, Robert. (2003). "Reforming Pakistan's Educational System: The Challenge of the Madrassas", *The Journal of Social, Political and Economic Studies,* 28(3): 257–274.

Malik, Jamal (ed.). (2008). *Madrasas in South Asia: Teaching Terror?* New York: Routledge.

Moosa, Ebrahim. (2015). *What is a Madrasa?* Chapel Hill: University of North Carolina Press.

Rahman, Tariq. (2008). "Madrasas: The Potential for Violence in Pakistan", in Jamal Malik (ed.), *Madrasas in South Asia: Teaching Terror?* London: Routledge, 61-85.

Rashid, Ahmed. (2000). *Taliban: Militant Islam, Oil and Fundamentalism in Central Asia.* New Haven: Yale University Press.

Rogan, Randall G. (2010). "Jihad Against Infidels and Democracy: A Frame Analysis of Jihadist Ideology and Jurisprudence for Martyrdom and Violent Jihad", *Communication Monographs,* 77(3): 393–413.

Saqib, Ghulam Nabi. (1983). *Modernization of Muslim Education in Egypt, Pakistan and Turkey: A Comparative Study.* Lahore: Islamic Book Service.

Shah, Jamal. (2012). "Zia-Ul-Haque and the Proliferation of Religion in Pakistan", *International Journal of Business and Social Science,* 3(21): 310–323.

Steven, Simon and Jonathan, Stevenson. (2009). "Afghanistan: How Much is Enough?", *Survival,* 51(5): 47–67. doi.org/10.1080/00396330903309857

World Bank. (February 2019). "Pakistan's Scarce Water Can Bring More Value to People and Economy". [Online]. Viewed from www.worldbank.org/en/ news/press-release/2019/02/04/pakistans-scarce-water-can-bring-more-value-to-people-and-economy [Date accessed October 10, 2019].

Zaman, Mohammed Qasim. (1999). "Religious Education and the Rhetoric of Reform: The Madrasa in British India and Pakistan", *Comparative Studies in Society and History,* 41(2): 294–323. doi.org/10.1017/S0010417599002091

PART IV
RELIGION MATTERS IN
CONFLICT RESOLUTION

7

ORIENTATION
WHAT DO THEY HAVE THAT OTHERS DON'T?

Christine Schliesser, S. Ayse Kadayifci-Orellana, and Pauline Kollontai

When violent interreligious conflict erupted in Kaduna, Nigeria, in 1992, Imam Muhammad Ashafa and Pastor James Wuye were drawn into the fighting, trying to kill each other in the name of religion. After the violence had stopped, the two religious leaders reluctantly agreed to meet. Over the years, they built a relationship with each other and agreed to join forces in helping to heal the chasm between their communities. They founded the Interfaith Mediation Centre in 1995, an interreligious grassroots organization that successfully promotes reconciliation and conflict resolution between Muslims and Christians in Nigeria. Meanwhile, their interfaith methodology for prospective civic peace activists is used in Africa and beyond.

While the example of Ashafa and Wuye illustrates religious peace-making within religious conflicts, other examples demonstrate the effectiveness of religious peacemaking also in transforming violent conflicts with no apparent religious dimensions. The engagement of the Catholic community of Sant'Egidio, for example, was vital in helping to end the civil war in Mozambique (1977–1992), a proxy war during the Cold War.

INCREASING RECOGNITION: RELIGION MATTERS IN CONFLICT RESOLUTION

Increasingly, scholars and practitioners are recognizing the role religion can play in addressing conflicts. Religion becomes a major factor in conflict and conflict resolution when, for instance, parties are defined along religious lines and where religion is an integral aspect of social and cultural life, as noted by Appleby (2001/1996), Gopin (2009), Sampson and Lederach (2000), Smock (2008), Abu-Nimer (2015), Lederach (1997), and Schliesser (2018). These scholars point out that religious traditions can bring moral, social, and spiritual resources to peacebuilding, and inspire a sense of engagement and commitment to the process. "Religion is a source not only of intolerance, human rights violations, and extremist violence, but also of nonviolent conflict transformation, the defense of human rights, integrity in government, and reconciliation and stability in divided societies" (Appleby 2001/1996: 821). Religious texts and prophetic stories provide examples of peacemaking, forgiveness, and compassion that can lead to a change of attitudes and behaviors, as well as encourage making peace with the "other". Religious values, principles (such as forgiveness, patience, mercy, accountability), and rituals can facilitate healing and trauma management.

The impact of religious peacemaking and conflict resolution is also more and more being taken into consideration at the international policy-making level. In July 2017, the UN Office on Genocide Prevention and the Responsibility to Protect launched a "Plan of Action for Religious Leaders and Actors to Prevent Incitement to Violence that Could Lead to Atrocity Crimes". In this Plan, UN Secretary General Guterres points out that "Religious leaders can play a particularly important role in influencing the behavior of those who share their beliefs" (UN 2017: Foreword), thereby recognizing them as significant agents in conflict and conflict resolution. In a similar vein, the 2018 UN and World Bank Study "Pathways to Peace" states: "The more successful cases [of conflict prevention] mobilized a coalition of domestic actors to influence incentives towards peace, bringing in the comparative advantages of civil society, including women's groups, the faith community, and the private sector to manage tensions" (UN and World Bank 2018: xxi).

So, while the role of religious actors in conflict resolution is increasingly recognized, the concrete contribution of religious actors remains opaque. What exactly is it about religious actors that makes the partnership with them seem significant? What are their specific characteristics and contributions to conflict resolution?

RELIGIOUS ACTORS IN CONFLICT RESOLUTION: CONTRIBUTIONS

Attempts at systematizing the potentials of religious actors face a number of difficulties. Besides the inherent ambivalence of religion itself, we need to consider the internal plurality of any given religion as well as the vast variety of religious actors and FBOs. Furthermore, FBOs differ in the way they relate faith and praxis. Ron Sider and Heidi Unruh developed a typology of six different types of FBOs active in development, ranging from faith-permeated development work to quasi-secular organizations (Sider and Unruh 2004).

While keeping the plurality of religious actors in mind, we can still point to certain characteristics and contributions common to many of these actors. Not all of these characteristics are exclusive in the sense that they only pertain to religious actors, nor does every religious actor display all of them. Below, we differentiate between "formal" and "material" contributions—even though the borderlines can be a bit blurry at times. In Chapter 3 we discussed six different ways of approaching religion in conflict, namely: religion as community, as a set of teachings, as spirituality, as practice, as discourse, and as an institution. Our intention behind this was to make the different dimensions of religion that can have an impact on a conflict situation more visible. In this chapter, we now shift our focus from religion in general to religious actors and their concrete contributions. To show how close both perspectives are connected, we link the specificities we found in religious actors with the six ways of approaching religion in conflict. Some of the characteristics we point out align with one of these dimensions, while others cut across different aspects or broaden a certain aspect.

Trust: religion as community, religion as practice

For religious actors to be effective peacebuilders, religious leaders, institutions, and discourses must be perceived as legitimate and credible by the parties involved in the conflict. Religious leaders and faith-based actors often enjoy a high degree of credibility and moral and spiritual legitimacy. This is especially visible in contexts such as Rwanda and Pakistan where religion plays a significant role in society. In the joint attendance of Sunday church services or Friday prayer and in the participation in youth groups or women's groups, religious and social activities merge.

At the same time, the trust enjoyed by religious actors is often-times linked to religion as practice because many FBOs have a long history of service addressing community needs. When Sant'Egidio was asked by the warring parties in Mozambique to mediate between them, it could not only draw on a web of relationships with locals, but also on a history of social services and catering to the urgent needs of the poor. The respect and trust associated with religious actors is furthermore connected to their perception as neutral agents. They are seen as not pursuing their own personal gain, but rather as committed to peace only (Bouta, Kadayifci-Orellana, and Abu-Nimer 2005). In the case of Sant'Egidio and Mozambique, the success of their mediation efforts therefore depended to a large degree on this community's record of friendship across boundaries and their own integrity.

Relationships and identity: religion as community

Connected to the level of trust and credibility they enjoy, religious actors often display strong relationship-building skills as "religious leaders are uniquely positioned to foster nonviolent conflict transformation through the building of constructive, collaborative relationships within and across ethnic and religious groups for the common good of the entire population of a region" (Appleby 2008: 127). Relationships are in turn innately connected to identity formation. It is through relationships—through the other—that we understand ourselves (Buber 1996). This specific ability of relationship building helps religious actors not only in building communities and forming identities, but also in playing a leading role in social change processes. Faith-based actors can move parties towards an agreement by building trust between disputants and by engaging the moral and spiritual resources that emphasize shared identities and experiences as well as common moral and spiritual values (Kadayifci-Orellana 2017).

For a better understanding of this specific characteristic of religious actors and of how it can foster sustainable conflict resolution, we found social network analysis helpful (Granovetter 1973). Social network analysis differentiates between "strong-ties groups" and "weak-ties groups", both of which impact our sense of identity. Strong-ties groups provide reliability and meaning to their members, who are closely connected to one another, for instance, in traditional villages or religious communities. Due to their self-referentiality and strong group coherence, however, new ideas often haven difficulties gaining a footing. Weak-ties groups, on the other hand, refer to communities with loose contact between their members, such as in chat groups. They are less reliable for the individual member, yet they allow for the rapid dissemination of new information and concepts. Religious actors often originate from strong-ties groups. Given their strong relationship-building skills, they are able to function as "connectors" between these groups (Gopin 2009: 79). This competency is of crucial importance in processes of social change. Successful conflict resolution needs nothing less than a paradigm change in thinking and behavior that in turn depends on the acceptance of new concepts in a given community. For this to be successful, connectors are necessary, that is, people who enjoy sufficient credibility in strong-ties groups to ensure that a new idea is not dismissed from the onset, while at the same time are able to quickly reach a large number of people. While it is well possible to stop immediate violence through outside intervention, sustainable peace cannot be had without relationship building within and between communities.

Networks: religion as an institution, religion as spirituality

Religious actors can often rely on well-organized, sometimes extensive networks, providing them with financial, institutional, and human resources. Religious leaders and organizations have access to community members through mosques, churches, temples, community centers, and educational institutions. In some cases, their involvement can bring international support from their sister organizations. Religious groups also tend to have a broader base than many secular NGOs. This broad base provides a wide pool of committed individuals who are willing to work as volunteers.

> Religious communities are, without question, the largest and best-organized civil institutions in the world today, claiming the allegiance of billions of believers and bridging the divides of race, class and nationality. They are uniquely equipped to meet the challenges of our time: resolving conflicts, caring for the sick and needy, promoting peaceful co-existence among all peoples.
>
> (World Conference on Religion and Peace,
> cited in Heist and Cnaan 2016: 6)

Next to a wider, sometimes national, or even international support structure, religious actors can rely on local, grassroot networks. Through their sermons, lectures, and educational programs, they can reach out to large number of people in their societies. As so-called "middle-range" leaders, they are often in a unique place to reach out to both grassroots and high-level leaderships. The ability to connect to and mobilize local members and congregations gives religious actors a strategic advantage over many secular NGOs. This ability becomes of crucial significance not least in the event of crises, be it conflict or natural disaster, as religious actors cannot only provide first-hand insight and information but can often help to connect international agents with local people well familiar with the language and culture, spirituality and discourse, as well as with the urgent needs and challenges in a particular situation.

Funding: religion as an institution, religion as spirituality

While part of the network discussion, funding deserves special attention. "Giving USA 2018" reports that even though charitable giving for international affairs decreased compared to the previous year, faith-based development organizations were still amongst the top recipients of aid money. Food for the Poor, for instance, received $ 987.6 million in private contributions; World Vision got

$786.01 million (*Giving USA 2018*). It is furthermore of interest to look at where the money comes from. Many faith-based and secular international development organizations accept financial support from governments, yet they differ in their approaches. While government support is often a major source of income for secular NGOs, FBOs tend to limit government support in order to maintain their independence (Smillie and Minear 2004). For many FBOs, the main source of the money comes from private sources, including collective donations, such as collected during a religious service. Various faith-based actors like Quakers, Sant'Egidio, and Islamic Relief Services have well-established regional and global networks to which they can turn for institutional and financial resources. Next to the community aspect, the spirituality dimension of religion becomes relevant. Different religions consider tithing, almsgiving, and charity an integral part of their tradition. Giving to the poor thus becomes an intrinsic part of one's own spirituality.

Services: religion as practice

To many religious actors, engaging in community service is an expression of the practice dimension of faith. When it comes to service delivery, studies find that both FBOs and secular NGOs provide similar services. While the kinds of services provided—including food provision, clean water, refugee services, education, orphanages, medical services, microfinance, or infrastructure—are similar, a recent study notes differences in the number of activities that these organizations are engaged in. FBOs were covering a wider range of services rather than specializing in certain areas as secular NGOs tend to. "Faith-based organizations on average provided significantly more kinds of services (4.2. types of services per organization) compared to the secular organizations (2.6 types per organization, $p < 0.05$)" (Heist and Cnaan 2016: 9). Further research is required, but the findings indicate a higher concern for holistic service provision on the side of FBOs.

Studies also show that numerous collaborations exist between NGOs and FBOs, as seen, for example, in Kano and Lagos states, Nigeria. The NGO BAOBAB focuses on women's human rights. Based in Lagos, BAOBAB has outreach teams in 14 states across Nigeria who work with Muslim FBOs with the aim of developing better understanding of women's rights in the context of Sharia. In Kano state, the Ganuwa Group comprises different NGOs, FBOs, and other interested parties who work together to promote HIV/AIDS awareness and prevention. The key reason for these collaborations "stem from increasing realization amongst NGOs and development agencies of the crucial role that FBOs can play in the delivery of programmes that have implications for the religious beliefs of target populations" (Davis et al. 2011: 38).

MATERIAL CONTRIBUTIONS OF RELIGIOUS ACTORS

Normative concepts and values: religion as a set of teachings, religion as practice

Religions are normative. They come with dogmatic claims (What is true?) and ethical implications (What is good?). Though often misused for the purpose of inciting violence and conflict, religious teachings also contain powerful normative concepts and values that can be used to further peace and reconciliation. Faith-based actors have a unique spiritual and moral leverage that is often unavailable to secular peacebuilders. Spiritual resources include values, principles, norms, and rituals rooted in religious traditions which can be used to encourage parties to embrace a new reality, change their behavior, and form new relationships with others, even with former enemies. The Christian tradition, for example, offers the concepts of forgiveness, grace, and love that encompasses even the enemy. By teaching love and reconciliation instead of hatred and exclusion, religious values are disseminated that call for concrete behavioral implications. The parable of the Good Samaritan (Luke 10:25–37) or the Sermon on the Mount (Matthew 5–7) have inspired countless Christians to work for peace and justice. Equally, the Jewish and Muslim traditions contain potent resources, including the concepts of love, compassion, forgiveness, and the pursuit of justice and doing good (Kadayifci-Orellana, Abu-Nimer, and Mohamed-Saleem 2013). These teachings serve not only as motivations for concrete actions, but also as ethical orientation and practice as they help to transform attitudes and stereotypes, as well as ways of thinking and acting.

Holistic perspective: religion as spirituality, religion as discourse

Religious actors usually bring a specific kind of anthropology, that is, understanding of the human person, as part of their discourse to the field, as they embrace a holistic perspective on well-being. This means that well-being relates not only to physical and material aspects, but to spiritual and emotional dimensions as well. Religious communities often provide care for the soul *and* for the body. Their holistic perspective gives them an advantage over many secular NGOs who focus primarily on material support. In postgenocide Rwanda, for example, Christian churches offer reconciliation initiatives linked with development projects, such as giving a cow to a victim and a perpetrator. Together, they care for the cow and share the income generated by selling its milk. Psychological and spiritual support of those affected by violence is supplemented here with practical help for daily life, resulting in welcome synergetic effects that enhance the sustainability of both kinds of efforts.

Meaning: religion as spirituality, religion as practice

Through their sacred narratives, spirituality, and practices, religious communities give meaning to everyday life. We want to illustrate this by pointing to the experience of Oledai, a village in Western Uganda, an area that experienced violent insurgency between 1986 and 1993. Oledai PAG (Pentecostal Assembly of God) Church was established in 1994, caring for both the spiritual and practical concerns of the community. At about the same time, different NGOs also moved in, supported by the $233 million worth World Bank-funded Northern Uganda Social Action Fund (NUSAF). The aim of these NGOs was to "empower communities … by enhancing their capacity to systematically identify, prioritise, and plan for their needs and implement sustainable development initiatives" (Manor 2007: 264). Ten years later, the NGOs and their initiatives had disappeared. Oledai Church, however, was flourishing, having more than quadrupled in size. How is this difference in impact to be explained? For anthropologist Ben Jones, the main criterion is meaning. While the NGOs remained extrinsic to the local community, Oledai Church successfully engaged the hearts and minds of its members, becoming part of the community and making its members feel at home. The NGOs' initiatives, on the other hand, displayed "mostly technical functions and represent an ideological agenda—of rights, empowerment or participation—that had little purchase. In a fundamental way the work of NGOs lacked meaning" (Jones 2012: 200).

Rituals: religion as spirituality, religion as practice

Rituals structure our daily life. Especially in times of turmoil, these rituals help to provide stability and meaning. Religious rituals like prayer and meditation can therefore become significant resources for support and inner structure, even as outer (political, economic, etc.) structures are collapsing or changing. Rituals and ceremonies in themselves are ambivalent, however. They can be employed to create insider-outsider boundaries and to encourage conflicts, such as the Rwandan génocidaires taking communion to strengthen themselves for their "work". Yet they can also be used as powerful resources for coping with conflict. Catholic communities in post-genocide Rwanda, for example, have creatively adapted the Christian Sacrament of Reconciliation. The *gacaca nkirisitu* (Christian gacaca) has thus become a ritualized pastoral process for perpetrators and survivors on their path to reconciliation (Carney 2015). In the context of overcoming conflict, religious rituals may thus be used, adapted, or created to help facilitate healing processes.

Dealing with trauma: religion as a set of teachings, religion as spirituality

The generation of meaning becomes all the more virulent during the experience and in the aftermath of atrocities. Due to gross violations of human rights and excessive violence, individuals and communities involved in conflict are usually traumatized and have deep injuries. These can be passed on to the next generations, resulting in intergenerational trauma. Painful memories of conflict, loss of loved ones, and injuries suffered cause deep emotional and psychological stress. Healing these injuries and trauma thus becomes a major component of peacebuilding efforts, especially for reconciliation at the grassroots level (Abu-Nimer and Kadayifci-Orellana 2008). For if these wounds are left unaddressed, they can not only result in severe post-traumatic stress disorder (PTSD), but also breed bitterness, hatred, and revenge, thereby perpetuating the spiral of violence as former victims turn into perpetrators.

Religious traditions and their emphasis on transformation and a new beginning can help to integrate experiences of loss and hurt into a framework that restores meaning. Religious perspectives offer hope and an eschatological horizon that assist traumatized victims in dealing with the past and the present. At the same time, concepts such as forgiveness and grace include powerful resources for dealing with guilt, shame, and failure, existential experiences inevitably encountered in the context of conflict and reconciliation on the side of both victims and perpetrators. In Islam, for example, Islamic values of peacebuilding, reestablishment of harmony and order, and respect for others, together with Islamic ideas on fate, predestination, and total sovereignty of God serve as the basis for healing and reconciliation (Abu-Nimer and Kadayifci-Orellana 2008). Organizations such as the Nigerian Interfaith Mediation Center focus on healing the trauma of injuries inflicted during times of conflict.

Memory and reconciliation: religion as a set of teachings, religion as spirituality, religion as practice

"Culture, history, memory, authenticity ... —these are the currency of the local peacebuilder" (Appleby 2008: 128). Of these, we would like to draw special attention to memory. During, but even more so after violence, questions of dealing with the past and of remembering arise. Without memory, there is no path to reconciliation and sustainable peace. How we remember the past, what we remember—and what we don't remember—has an impact on how we live in the present and the future. Yet memory is not ethically neutral. Rather, it can be just or unjust, as Paul Ricœur's (2004: 68) call for a "juste mémoire" ("just memory") reminds us. A just memory does not simply mirror the victors' narrative but includes the victims' perspectives.

Nevertheless, remembrance in itself and as the mere representation of the past rarely leads to a genuine new beginning. For this, concepts such as forgiveness and reconciliation are helpful, even if not always possible. Forgiveness liberates both victim and perpetrator from the haunting past—and from each other. Through forgiveness, the victim regains self-determination over his/her own life, while the perpetrator is no longer defined merely by his/her deeds but acknowledged in his/her shared humanity. As genuinely religious concepts, forgiveness and reconciliation can be actively strengthened through the teaching and practice of FBOs, religious actors, and communities, as displayed, for example, by Christian churches in post-genocide Rwanda. Forgiving does not mean forgetting, nor does it mean impunity. Yet it can pave the way for the genuine healing of relationships and communities as prerequisites for sustainable peace.

In this chapter, we gave an orientation on some of the specific characteristics and contributions—both formal and material—associated with religious actors in conflict resolution. While religious actors have no magic wand to solve conflicts and while their role must not be overstated, it is clear that they bring significant resources to the field that no one genuinely interested in conflict resolution can afford to ignore. The following case studies illustrate the specific contributions of religious actors in concrete contexts of violent conflict.

REFERENCES

Abu-Nimer, Mohammed. (2015). "Religion and Peacebuilding: Reflections on Current Challenges and Future Prospects", *Journal of Interreligious Studies,* 16: 14–29.

Abu-Nimer, Mohammed and S. Ayse Kadayifci-Orellana. (2008). "Muslim Peace Building Actors in Africa and the Balkans", *Peace and Change,* 33(4): 549–581.

Appleby, R. Scott. (2001/1996). "Religion as an Agent of Conflict Transformation and Peace Building", in C.A. Crocker, F.O. Hampson, and P. Aall (eds.), *Turbulent Peace: The Challenges of Managing International Conflict.* Washington DC: United States Institute of Peace Press, 821–840.

Appleby, R. Scott. (2008). "Building Sustainable Peace: The Roles of Local and Transnational Religious Actors", in Thomas Banchoff (ed.), *Religious Pluralism, Globalization, and World Politics.* Oxford: Oxford University Press, 125–154.

Bouta, Tsjeard, S. Ayse Kadayifci-Orellana, and Mohammed Abu-Nimer. (2005). *Faith-Based Peace-Building: Mapping and Analysis of Christian, Muslim, and Faith-Based Actors.* The Hague: Clingendael Institute.

Buber, Martin. (1996) *I and Thou* (trans. by Walter Kaufmann). New York: Simon & Schuster.

Carney, James J. (2015). "A Generation After Genocide: Catholic Reconciliation in Rwanda", *Theological Studies,* 76(4): 785–812.

Cavanaugh, William T. (2004). "Sins of Omission: What 'Religion and Violence' Arguments Ignore", *The Hedgehog Review: Critical Reflections on Contemporary Culture,* 6(1): 34–50.

Davis, Comfort, Jedgede, Ayodele, Leurs, Robert, Sunmola, Adegbenga, and Ukiwo, Ukoha. (2011). Comparing Religious and Secular NGOs in Nigeria: Are Faith-Based Organizations Distinctive?, Working Paper, Religion and Development Research Programme, International Development Department, University of Birmingham.

Garred, Michelle and Mohammed, Abu-Nimer. (2018). "Introduction", in Michelle Garred and Mohammed Abu-Nimer (eds.), *Making Peace with Faith: The Challenges of Religion and Peacebuilding.* New York: Rowman and Littlefield, 1–26.

Giving USA Foundation. (2018). *Giving USA 2018: The Annual Report on Philanthropy for the Year 2017.* Chicago: Giving USA Foundation. Viewed from https://lclsonline.org/wp-content/uploads/2018/12/Giving-USA-2018-Annual-Report.pdf [Date accessed October 31, 2019].

Gopin, Marc. (2009). *To Make the Earth Whole: The Art of Citizen Diplomacy in an Age of Religious Militancy.* Lanham, MD: Roman & Littlefield.

Granovetter, Marc. (1973). "The Strength of Weak Ties", *American Journal of Sociology,* 78(1): 1360–1380.

Hayward, Susan. (2012). *Religion and Peacebuilding. Reflections on Current Challenges and Future Prospects.* United States Institute of Peace Special Report. Washington, DC. Viewed from www.usip.org/sites/default/files/SR313.pdf [Date accessed October 31, 2019].

Heist, Dan and Cnaan, Ram A. (2016). "Faith-Based International Development Work: A Review", *Religion,* 7(19): 1–17.

Jones, Ben. (2012). "Pentecostalism, Development NGOs and Meaning", in Dena Freeman (ed.), *Pentecostalism and Development: Churches, NGOs and Social Change in Africa.* London: Palgrave Macmillan, 181–202.

Kadayifci-Orellana, S. Ayse. (2009). "Ethno-Religious Conflicts: Exploring the Role of Religion in Conflict Resolution", in Jacob Bercovitch, Victor Kremenyuk, and I. William Zartman (eds.), *The SAGE Handbook of Conflict Resolution.* Los Angeles: SAGE, 264–284.

Kadayifci-Orellana, S. Ayse. (2017). "Religion and Mediation: Strange Bedfellows or Natural Allies?", in Alexia Georgakopoulos (ed.), *The Handbook of Mediation: Theory, Research and Practice.* New York: Routledge, 369–378.

Kadayifci-Orellana, S. Ayse, Abu-Nimer, Mohammed, and Mohamed-Saleem, Amjad. (2013). "Understanding an Islamic Framework for Peacebuilding", Islamic Relief Worldwide, Working Paper Series No. 201302. Birmingham, UK. Viewed from http://library.iracademy.org.uk/understanding-an-islamic-framework-for-peacebuilding/ [Date accessed October 31, 2019].

Lederach , John Paul. (1997). *Building Peace: Sustainable Reconciliation in Divided Societies.* Washington, DC: USIP Press.

Mandaville, Peter and Nozell, Melissa. (August 2017). *Engaging Religion and Religious Actors in Countering Violent Extremism*. United States Institute of Peace, Washington, DC. Viewed from www.usip.org/sites/default/files/ SR413-Engaging-Religion-and-Religious-Actors-in-Countering-Violent-Extremism.pdf [Date accessed October 31, 2019].

Manor, James. (2007). *Aid That Works: Successful Development in Fragile States*, Washington, DC: World Bank 2007. Viewed from http://documents. worldbank.org/curated/en/969871468336614487/pdf/379590REVISED01 OFFICIAL0USE0ONLY1.pdf [Date accessed October 31, 2019].

Marshall, Katherine, Hayward, Susan, Zambra, Claudia, Breger, Esther, and Jackson, Sarah. (2011). *Women in Religious Peacebuilding*, Washington, DC: United States Institute of Peace. Viewed from www.usip.org/publications/ 2011/05/women-religious-peacebuilding [Date accessed October 31, 2019].

Ricœur, Paul. (2004). *Memory, History, Forgetting* (trans. by Kathleen Blamey and David Pellauer). Chicago: University of Chicago Press.

Sampson, Cynthia and Lederach, John Paul (eds.). (2000). *From the Ground Up: Mennonite Contributions to International Peacebuilding*. New York: Oxford University Press.

Schliesser, Christine. (2018). "From 'A Theology of Genocide' To A 'Theology of Reconciliation'? On the Role of Christian Churches in the Nexus of Religion and Genocide in Rwanda", *Religions*. Special Issue: Religion and Genocide, 9(34): 1–14.

Sider, Ron and Unruh, Heidi R. (2004). "Typology of Religious Characteristics of Social Service and Educational Organizations and Programs", *Nonprofit and Voluntary Sector Quarterly,* 33(1): 109–134.

Smillie, Ian and Minear, Larry. (2004). *The Charity of Nations. Humanitarian Action in a Calculating World*. Bloomfield, CT: Kumarian Press.

Smock, David. (2008). Religion in World Affairs. Its Role in Conflict and Peace, United States Institute of Peace Special Report. Viewed from www.usip.org/ publications/2008/02/religion-world-affairs-its-role-conflict-and-peace

United Nations and World Bank. (2018). *Pathways for Peace: Inclusive Approaches to Preventing Violent Conflict*, Washington, DC. Viewed from https:// openknowledge.worldbank.org/handle/10986/28337. [Date accessed October 31, 2019].

United Nations Office on Genocide Prevention and the Responsibility to Protect. (2017). *Plan of Action for Religious Leaders and Actors to Prevent Incitement to Violence that Could Lead to Atrocity Crimes*, Washington, DC. Viewed from www.un.org/en/genocideprevention/documents/Plan%20 of%20Action%20Advanced%20Copy.pdf [Date accessed October 31, 2019].

8

JEWISH PERSPECTIVE
RELIGION IN ISRAEL'S QUEST FOR CONFLICT RESOLUTION AND RECONCILIATION IN ITS LAND RIGHTS CONFLICTS

Pauline Kollontai

INTRODUCTION: POLITICAL APPROACHES TO RESOLVING LAND CONFLICTS

Seventy-one years on from its establishment, Israel continues to be in conflict over land with the Negev Bedouin and the Palestinians. During these past seven decades there have been signs of a reduction in the level and intensity of these conflicts. In the case of the Negev Bedouin, the first serious attempt at addressing this issue was seen in the work of the Goldberg Commission, set up by the Israeli government in 2007 during the Prime Ministership of Ehud Olmet. The Goldberg Commission, chaired by retired Supreme Court Justice, Eliezer Goldberg, had eight members, including two Bedouin representatives. The starting point for Goldberg was to acknowledge that there had been a number of government committees tasked to propose further strategies for Negev Bedouin resettlement and to find a compromise over land, "Most of these committees have had no serious impact on the issues they were set up to deal with" (Goldberg 2011: 22). At the beginning of the Commission's Report it states that seeing the Bedouin as the "other" has to be changed, "The approach of 'us' and 'them' is not acceptable to us, and it will not advance a solution, but rather drive it further away"

(Goldberg 2011: 5). This approach is also a fundamental obstacle to resolving Israel's conflict with the Palestinians. As of the time of writing (September 2019), there has been no significant improvement to the Negev Bedouin's land struggle with the Israeli state.

Attempts at finding ways to resolve the situation with the Palestinians have been evident amongst some political leaders since the 1970s from the two main parties—Likud and Labour. There are two key examples of this. The first under the leadership of Menachem Begin with a proposal for "Home Rule" for Palestinians in Judea, Samaria, and Gaza in the late 1970s. This became part of the discussions at the Camp David Accords aimed to facilitate dialogue between Israel and Egypt through the offices of the American President Jimmy Carter. The peace framework agreed at Camp David proposed that a self-governing authority for Palestinians in the West Bank would be set up; Israeli troops are to withdraw from the West Bank and Gaza after an election of a Palestinian self-governing authority to replace Israel's military government. This has only been partially realized. The second example is the Oslo Accords in 1993 signed by Yasar Arafat, Chairman of the Palestinian Liberation Organization (PLO), and Israeli Prime Minister Yitzhak Rabin. In summary, The Declaration of Principles deemed it essential to begin the process of resolving the Israeli–Palestinian conflict. Unfortunately, by 1996 these accords had stalled and eventually collapsed due to a variety of factors on both sides, including the assassination of the Israeli Prime Minister Rabin at a Peace Rally in Tel Aviv by Yigal Amir, an Israeli Jew who opposed the Rabin's overall peace plan on religious grounds. As with many enlightened moments in human history the full expression of making the necessary changes to deep conflict is not quickly and easily implemented. Since the mid-1990s, conflict over Palestinian rights to the land and their call for independent statehood has either continued to stagnate or has actually deteriorated.

RELIGION IN THE SEARCH FOR CONFLICT RESOLUTION AND RECONCILIATION: CAN RELIGION HELP?

Overcoming the viewpoint that Bedouin and Palestinians are the "other" requires more than passing policies and legislation. In a state that claims to have a secular and religious identity, what can religion do to assist in developing, enhancing, and sustaining a society which gives justice and fairness to all?

In the Jewish tradition, the key resources that I would consider to be an essential tool in helping to resolve Israel's land conflicts is the Jewish ethical approach to the just treatment of the "other" or "stranger". The Jewish philosopher Hermann Cohen makes an important observation relevant to the discussion here. He considers the biblical injunction to treat the stranger as one's own citizen is an attempt to overcome prejudice by evoking sympathy which he believes can make an important contribution. But he argues that if the appeal to love employed by religion is the primary foundation of the ethical command to care for the stranger, then, on the basis of the hostility to strangers, which he witnessed in Germany at the beginning of the 20th century, this had made little impact on humanity. His approach is to disqualify love as a basis for ethical action and instead promotes a reinterpretation of love of the other (stranger, neighbor) in terms of the law (Cohen 1907: 216). However, trying to construct an ethics of the love of the stranger only through legal requirements and enforcement does not necessarily nurture human attributes of compassion, love, respect, mutual understanding, and empathy. It is not only about adhering to a legal instruction but it is given in the context that the values of compassion, justice, and peace are essential aspects of being human and that such values are also a necessary part of establishing and maintaining human relations that seek to enable the well-being of all people.

Can Judaism contribute to resolving Israel's conflict over land with the Palestinians and its Arab citizens? In considering this question there follows a brief overview of key Jewish teachings relevant to practicing constructive attitudes and behavior towards others which are essential in reducing conflict and promoting understanding and reconciliation. We will consider the work of two Israeli organizations/groups, namely: *Wahat al-Salam—Neve Shalom* (Oasis of Peace), a community of people living together, and Rabbis for Human Rights.

NORMATIVE CONCEPTS AND VALUES: RELIGION AS A SET OF TEACHINGS, RELIGION AS PRACTICE

The values of *Va'ahavtem et ha-Ger* (love of stranger) and *Ve'ahabhath le-Re'akha* (love of neighbor), as contained in the Hebrew scriptures, are an extremely important and significant set of teachings in this discussion. This duty of love of stranger is spoken about 36 times in the Hebrew scriptures, the best known of these teachings is in the Book of Leviticus:

> When a stranger resides with you in your land, you shall not wrong him. The stranger who resides with you shall be to as one of your citizens; you shall love him as yourself, for you were strangers in the land of Egypt: I the Lord am your God.
>
> (Lev. 19:33–34)

This teaching clearly states that if a non-Jew has come to live and work in a Jewish land then they are to be treated equally, without discrimination; they are to be treated as an equal citizen. Further reference to treating the stranger as one of your own citizens is present in the later teaching of Leviticus: "You shall have one standard of law for the stranger and the citizen alike" (Lev. 24:22), and in Numbers 15:16, which is referring specifically to the stranger who wishes to present a fire offering to God, it states, "There shall be one law for you and the resident stranger; it shall be a law for all time throughout the ages", and the basis of this teaching is that, "You and the stranger shall be alike before the Lord" (Numbers 15:15). The underpinning principle in this teaching is justice. The importance of not oppressing the stranger and practicing justice towards them appears in various places in Deuteronomy.

As with the treatment of the stranger, numerous teachings appear in the Hebrew scriptures of both a legal and ethical nature, aimed at providing a code of behavior covering all aspects of relations between neighbors. While there is not sufficient space to deal with this in depth here, it is worth considering key aspects of these teachings. The emphasis on being truthful, fair treatment, and not thinking or practicing evil against a neighbor is found in a number of the texts, including in the Book of Zechariah (Zech. 8:16–17). These teachings are considered to be encapsulated in the command: "Thou shalt love thy neighbor as thyself" (Lev. 19:18). Both Rabbi Hillel (110 BCE–10 CE) and Rabbi Akiba (40-137 CE) taught that the fundamental principle of the Torah is the Leviticus commandment: "Thou shalt love thy neighbor as thyself" (Ginzberg 1906: 1034; Finkelstein 1936: 210). Ben Azzai, a

student of Akiba, commented on the same commandment emphasizing the importance of love for all humankind because "all human
beings are descended from Adam, a common ancestor which means
being bound together by the kinship of a common origin" (Cohen
2008: 225). More recent articulation of Akkiba's understanding is
seen in the writings of 18th-century Rabbi and Kabbalist, Pinchas
Elijah Hurwitz, who argues that the core essence of love of
neighbor consists of loving all of humankind because of their identical humanity (Hurwitz 1818). During the 20th century a number
of Jewish thinkers also argued that the command concerning love
of neighbor must apply to non-Jews (Cohen 1907; Buber 1958;
Katz 1961).

Even if the Palestinians and Negev Bedouin are considered as
strangers—then, surely the admonishment "you shall not wrong the
stranger who lives alongside you" means they should be accorded
fair treatment, including recognizing where possible land claims or
adequate financial/land reparations on a level that would be given
to any Jewish citizens. Unfortunately, there continue to be those
within the current Jewish establishment in Israel that certainly do
not agree with this approach. An example was witnessed in 2010
with the views of Rabbi Ovadia Yosef, the former Sephardi Chief
Rabbi of Israel and then current Head of the Council of Torah
Sages and spiritual leader of Israel's ultra-orthodox Shas party. In
a Saturday night sermon, some of which was audio recorded and
later broadcast on Israel's Channel 10, Yosef said in relation to the
issues of what work non-Jews can perform on the Sabbath, "Goyim
(non-Jews) were born only to serve us. Without that, they have
no place in the world; only to serve the People of Israel" (Oyster
2010: 1). Challenges to such views of Rabbi Yosef in religious
circles come mostly from the Reform and Liberal religious communities in Israel. The next sections discuss how the Jewish values
of love and care for stranger and neighbor are being promoted and
actioned by various religious groups in Israel by focusing on the
work of Rabbis for Human Rights, founded in 1988, consisting of
Israeli rabbis and rabbinical students, and the community *Wahat al-
Salam—Neve Shalom*, jointly established by Jewish and Palestinian
Arab citizens of Israel in the 1970s, located between Jerusalem and
Tel Aviv.

TRUST: RELIGION AS COMMUNITY, RELIGION AS DISCOURSE

During the early stages of the first Palestinian Intifada, a small group of Israeli rabbis founded the organization, Rabbis for Human Rights (RHR). It consists of Israeli rabbis and rabbinical students from different streams of Judaism. RHR states: "We derive our authority from our Jewish tradition and the Universal Declaration of Human Rights. Our mission is to inform the Israeli public about human rights violations, and to pressure the state institutions to redress these injustices" (RHR 2019: 1). The work of this organization is identified as being located in the traditional Jewish responsibility of caring for and protecting the stranger, the poor, the weak, and the convert. In the run-up to voting in the 2015 Israeli election campaign, RHR released several public statements identifying these Jewish responsibilities as an essential aspect to voting. Rabbi Arik Ascherman referred to Torah teachings that condemn oppression and mistreatment of the "stranger". The overall message was about "Encouraging citizens to vote and reminding them to bring the values of human rights work and the honouring of God's Image along with them into the voting booth" (RHR 2015: 1).

There are six main areas of RHR's work, three of these are concerned specifically with Palestinian rights in the occupied territories and rights of Bedouin communities located in the Negev and Jahalin Bedouin communities situated on the outskirts of Jerusalem. In the occupied territories, human rights work, legal advocacy/intervention regarding land and other socio-economic rights, and aiming to protect agricultural access for Palestinian farmers is the core of their work. Their work with the Bedouin is advocating and petitioning against their forced displacement from land, resolving outstanding land claims, and in the Jahalin Bedouin community they provide children with afterschool and summer school activities. The three other areas of RHR's work involve providing advice and legal representation for any Israeli citizens with regard to socio-economic and welfare rights; human rights education workshops for post-secondary and university students to learn and understand about the importance of human rights in the Jewish tradition and interfaith work to "harness the teachings and values of our region's faiths as a means of reconciliation & understanding" (RHR 2019: 1).

NETWORKS, SERVICES, AND ADVOCACY: RELIGION AS INSTITUTION AND PRACTICE

RHR's work in the occupied territories involves trying to prevent and reverse the taking of Palestinian land by the Israeli state for Jewish settlers or other government projects; intervention to maintain road access for small Palestinian communities in Hebron, and protection of Palestinian rights who live amongst the large, growing Jewish settlements in parts of Hebron. Sometimes members of RHR's engage in nonviolent activism to reinforce the Jewish message of caring for and protecting all people. A recent example of this is seen in early 2019 in the Israeli-administered H2 area of Hebron, with a solidarity walk organized by RHR to speak with Palestinians, the Israeli military, and Jewish settlers about the growing harassment which Palestinians and their civilian international accompaniers have been facing from settlers and soldiers. Although there have been some signs hinting at a reduction in the level of harassment, RHR members continue to visit this area and aim to promote dialogue and understanding between the various communities by appealing to key Jewish ethical teachings in human relations. The work of RHR regarding the land rights and displacement of Negev Bedouin and the Jahalin Bedouin is done in collaboration with the Regional Council of Unrecognized Bedouin Villages and the Negev Coexistence Forum. It involves legal advice and advocacy, petitioning government to address and resolve these land injustices, public statements, organizing nonviolent activist events, and visiting these communities to show solidarity. A key focus of RHR's work since 2012 is ongoing public critique of the failure of government to implement the more positive elements of the Goldberg Commission's Report. Instead, they continue to block land arrangements for the majority of Bedouin land claims which total 590,000 dunams, refuse to give building permits even in recognized Bedouin villages, continue demolition of some villages, and there is a new development of Jewish towns on existing Bedouin land where Bedouins already live. Overall, the central message taken from the Jewish tradition in all RHR work is the sanctity of all human life, sanctifying the name of God through respect and care for all humanity, behaving ethically, and pursuing justice and peace.

IDENTITY, RELATIONSHIPS, AND HEALING: RELIGION AS COMMUNITY, RELIGION AS SPIRITUALITY

In an area between Jerusalem and Tel Aviv is located *Wahat al-Salam—Neve Shalom*, a community jointly established by Jewish and Palestinian Arab (Muslim and Christian) citizens of Israel. It was established in 1970 by Bruno Hussar, who was born in Egypt in 1911 to non-practicing Jewish parents. His early years were spent in Hungary, Italy, and Paris where, at the age of 39, having earlier converted to Christianity, he was ordained in 1950 as a Catholic Priest of the Dominican Order. Fr. Bruno Hassar never lost sense of his Jewish origins and in 1953 he went to live as a Dominican Priest in Israel. Here, over the next few years, after witnessing the growing fear and hatred between Jews and Arabs, he negotiated to have the *Wahat al-Salam—Neve Shalom* (WASNS) community established in 1970 on land belonging to the Latrun Monastery. This community of Jews, Christians, and Muslims live together and are dedicated to building justice, peace, and equality for all people in Israel and the wider region. Most of those living in the community regard religious belief as a personal matter, a part of cultural identity. In 2019 there are 70 families living in the community and it is expected to grow over the new few years to around 150 families (WASNS 2019a).

This community endeavors to provide "a model of equality, mutual respect and partnership that challenges existing patterns of racism and discrimination as well as the continued conflict" and many of its members work on peace, justice, and reconciliation projects in wider Israeli and Palestinian societies (WASNS 2019b: 1). To promote, nurture, and embed the key ideals and behavior of justice, peace, and equality for all people within its community and to take this to the wider society, the *Wahat al-Salam—Neve Shalom* community has its own kindergarten and primary school, both of which have a bilingual and multi-cultural curriculum (which includes religion). There has been increasing interest from some parents in the surrounding Gezer region who in 2018 "waged a struggle, including a protest with a one day hunger strike" to get the mayor of the Gezer region to allow their children to attend the WASNS kindergarten for their compulsory kindergarten year. Permission was eventually given and children and parents from outside experienced WASNS work and aims (WASNS 2018: 1). Teachers at the kindergarten and school receive ongoing additional training and guidance to support their work in delivering a bilingual and multi-cultural curriculum.

SERVICES, NETWORKS, AND TRUST BUILDING: RELIGION AS PRACTICE, RELIGION AS COMMUNITY

WASNS has a School of Peace (SFP) providing opportunities for adults from both within as well as outside the community to experience various forms of educational and practical projects. One of these is the Mixed Cities Program designed to focus on the challenges of the ongoing conflict between Israel and its Arab population and the Israeli–Palestinian conflict. In 2018 there were 22 participants from Jewish, Muslim, and Christian backgrounds working on five joint projects which they would continue to work together on back in their own respective communities. The Peace School also offers a new programme of seminars to facilitate dialogue and work between academic researchers and leaders of NGOs. In 2018, over 70 people attended this new programme, who aim to promote peace activism and the development of a shared society, particularly amongst students and young people back in the communities where they live and work (WASNS 2018: 2). Each year workshops are run for non-WASNS teachers designed to develop inter-group dialogue and negotiation skills. In 2018, over 30 participants attended the summer workshops coming from Jewish, Muslim, and Christian backgrounds and from other parts of the region around Jerusalem and Tel Aviv. Some of those who attended spoke of learning to realize that: "We are almost identical in everything: pain, feelings, emotions, we understand everything when we open up and hear the experiences of others" (WASNS 2018: 2). The encounter which the workshops enable between educationalists is spoken of as providing hope and optimism for the future, "that in another 70 years our grandchildren and great-grandchildren will sing a common anthem" (WASNS 2018: 2). Overall, the workshops show the importance of education as a tool to assist in building inclusive societies and remove barriers, "Even if we are not the ones in power, we are an essential part of society and everything starts with education and from educators" (WASNS 2018: 2). Other SFP work includes providing three-day youth encounter programmes for Arab and Jewish students from schools around the area; the Massa-Masar programme, started in 2015, bringing together Jewish, Muslim, and Christian teenagers over a four-day period. Through seminars and workshops that involve outdoor environmental activities and cultural encounters, participants can explore self and identity in relation to issues of religion, identity, and Jewish-Arab relations. One of the participants reflected what many of those who attended felt: "This Journey changed me. I will always ask questions. I will try to help everyone. I don't promise but I will listen and try. It is important to hear before you judge" (WASNS 2015: 3).

CONCLUSION

Principles of justice and peace are an essential part of the Jewish prophetic tradition and its ethical and legal frameworks. The living out of these values is identified in the Torah as central to the covenantal relationship between God and his chosen people. The context in which these commandments are given is of a people who have fled from slavery in Egypt and are on a journey to a land which God is said to have given them (Deut. 4:14, NIV). But going into a land that is already the land of other people who then are driven out or slaughtered, apparently on the command of God, raises somewhat of a dilemma in the current discussion of the land issues in contemporary Israel. It is therefore essential to recognize the diversity of the Jewish system of values and that interpreting and implementing these needs to be contextualized in the socio-political-historical moment of human life and experience (Jacobs 1960: 8–9). Therefore, can Judaism contribute to resolving Israel's conflict over land with the Palestinians and its Arab citizens? I would suggest that the Jewish tradition, as expressed and understood in the examples of the organizations discussed above, does have an important role and contribution to make. It will not be an easy task challenging the political and religious mindsets who believe that Israel has a right to rule the occupied territories, to oppress Palestinians, and continue to pursue an assimilation policy to homogenize Israel's non-Jewish citizens. But the Jewish tradition has evolved over the centuries through the dialogue, disagreement, and debate by Rabbis and scholars over interpretation of Jewish ethical and legal traditions in the context of their day. The challenge is to continue this process so that the Jewish ethical teachings of love and care for all humankind will be reasserted over the "nationalist and isolationist understanding of Jewish tradition" that dominates Israeli society (RHR 2019: 1).

REFERENCES

Buber, Martin. (1958). *I and Thou* (2nd rev. ed.). London: T&T Clark.

Cohen, Abraham. (2008). *Everyman's Talmud: The Teachings of the Rabbinic Sages.* New York: BN Publishing.

Cohen, Hermann. (1907). *Religion of Reason: Out of the Sources of Judaism.* New York: Scholars Press.

Finkelstein, Louis. (1936). *Akiba: Scholar, Saint and Martyr.* Viewed from https://archive.org/details/MN40169ucmf_3 [Date accessed September 20, 2019].

Ginzberg, Louis. (1906). "Akiba Ben Joseph", in *Jewish Encyclopaedia.* Viewed from http://jewishencyclopedia.com/articles/1033-akiba-ben-joseph [Date accessed September 20, 2019].

Goldberg, Eliezer. (2011). *Goldberg Commission's Recommendations,* The Regional Council for the Unrecognized Villages in the Negev. Viewed from www.landpedia.org/landdoc/Analytical_materials/Goldberg_recommendations-english.pdf [Date accessed April 10, 2019].

Hurwitz, Phinehas Elijah. (1818). *Sefer Ha-Berit.* Vilna: Menahem Man.

Jacobs, Louis. (1960). *Jewish Values.* Eugene, OR: Wipf & Stock.

Katz, Jacob. (1961). *Studies in Jewish-Gentile Relations in Medieval and Modern Times.* New Jersey: Oxford University Press/Behrman House Inc.

Oyster, Marc. (2010). "Sephardi Leader Yosef: Non-Jews Exist to Serve Jews", *Jewish Telegraphic Agency.* Viewed from www.jta.org/2010/10/18/news-opinion/israel-middle-east/sephardi-leader-yosef-non-Jews-exist-to-serve-jews [Date accessed October 18, 2010].

Rabbis for Human Rights (RHR). (2015). "Israeli Elections 2015: Who Will Stop the Cruel Abuse of El-Araqib and the Rest of the Negev Bedouin?" Press Release February 19, 2015. Viewed from https://rhr.org.il/eng/2015/02/israeli-elections-2015-who-will-stop-the-cruel-abuse-of-el-araqib-the-rest-of-the-negev-bedouin/ [Date accessed July 25, 2019].

Rabbis for Human Rights (RHR). (2019). "About Us". Viewed from https://rhr.org.il/eng/about/ https://rhr.org.il/eng/about/ [Date accessed July 30, 2019].

Wahat al-Salam—Neve Shalom (WASNS). (2015). "Massa-Masr ('Journey')—an Exciting Programme for Jewish, Muslim and Christian Young People". Oasis of Peace. Viewed from www.wasns.org/massa-masar-journey-2015 [Date accessed June 27, 2019].

Wahat al-Salam—Neve Shalom (WASNS). (2018). "Summer 2018 Newsletter". Oasis of Peace. Viewed from www.wasns.org/summer-2018-newsletter [Date accessed June 20, 2019].

Wahat al-Salam—Neve Shalom (WASNS). (2019a). "Community". Oasis of Peace. Viewed from www.wasns.org/-community- [Date accessed June 24, 2019].

Wahat al-Salam—Neve Shalom (WASNS). (2019b). *Various Information and Documents about Wahat al-Salam—Neve Shalom*. Viewed from www.wasns.org/ [Date accessed July 24, 2019].

9

CHRISTIAN PERSPECTIVE

RELIGION IN POST-GENOCIDE RWANDA'S QUEST FOR CONFLICT RESOLUTION AND RECONCILIATION

Christine Schliesser

INTRODUCTION: THE CONTEXT

On April 6, 1994, the plane carrying Rwandan President Juvénal Habyarimana and Cyprien Ntaryamira, the president of Burundi, was shot down as it approached Kigali, capital of Rwanda. Everyone on board was killed. While the question of responsibility remains disputed until today, this attack served as the catalyst for the genocide in Rwanda. Since 1990, Rwanda had suffered under a civil war. With the attack on the plane, civil war culminated in the well-prepared massacre of up to one million children, women and men, while the world community stood by and watched (Dallaire 2004). Most of the victims belonged to the Tutsi minority (ca. 15 percent), yet countless moderate Hutu (ca. 85 percent) who refused to participate in the killings were murdered as well. What became the fastest genocide of modern history stood out not only because of its preventability, systematic preparation and brevity, but also because of its cruelty. Many victims were cut into pieces with machetes or buried alive. Due to the excessive sexual violence in the Rwandan genocide, sexual violence and mutilation has since become acknowledged and punishable as genocidal crimes

("Akayesu ruling" of 1998). Another characteristic of the Rwandan genocide is that many victims and perpetrators knew each other. They were neighbors, friends, or even family.

Convicted perpetrators, who have been released from prison, usually return to their home villages, oftentimes the place of their atrocities and the home of survivors. There, feelings of hatred and fear, shame and revenge, are all mingled together. With a country virtually in ashes, the struggle for everyday survival was compounded by the emotional turmoil of both survivors and perpetrators wrestling with anxiety and hostility. Rwanda's long-term president Paul Kagame realized that in order for the country to be rebuilt, he needed to provide stability and social unity. He thus initiated a "National Politics of Reconciliation", pushing reconciliation initiatives on all levels in society. On a national level, Rwanda's "National Unity and Reconciliation Commission" (NURC) was founded that promotes different reconciliation and sensitization projects throughout the country. The terms "Tutsi", "Hutu", and "Twa" were forbidden, and the official motto "We are all Rwandan" was introduced to forge a new, national identity. On the judicial level, Rwanda established the so-called gacaca courts, traditional mechanisms of conflict resolution. In terms of stability and economic progress, Kagame's reconciliation strategy seems to be paying off as Rwanda's Human Development Index (HDI) has steadily increased and foreign investors hail Rwanda's "economic miracle" (Amman 2015: 31). At the same time, however, reports of severe and continuing violations of human rights and of a political climate that stifles basic rights, such as freedom of the press and freedom of political opposition, give rise to concern (Bouka 2018).

WHAT HAPPENED TO RELIGION AFTER THE GENOCIDE?

A hundred days of slaughter in 1994 left Rwanda permanently altered. The effects of the genocide were not only visible on the social, economic, and political levels, Rwanda's religious landscape changed as well. With about 90 percent Christians, pre-genocide Rwanda was—and still is—one of the most Christian countries on the African continent. Within the Christian faith, it was Catholicism that was most prominent with almost two-thirds of the population following the Catholic faith. Different from other African countries, the wave of Christian revival and renewal that had swept across Africa at the end of the 20th century had bypassed Rwanda to a large extent.

It was only after the genocide that these "new" churches experienced any kind of significant growth in Rwanda. While the once dominant Catholic Church lost almost one-third of its members, Protestant churches doubled their membership numbers from 19 percent pre-genocide to 38 percent post-genocide (National Institute of Statistics of Rwanda 2014: xv). Most of this increase can be attributed to new churches of Pentecostal and charismatic orientation. Pentecostal and charismatic churches place special emphasis on a personal relationship with God through accepting Jesus Christ as personal Lord and Savior and on spiritual gifts such as speaking in tongues and divine healing. With their emphasis on healing, on breaking with the past, and a new beginning, Pentecostal churches seem to hearken to the needs of a society traumatized by mass violence. It was oftentimes through refugees returning from exile that these new churches were introduced to the country.

Contributing further to the change of the religious landscape after the genocide was a sense of disillusion and disappointment with the established churches, especially with the Catholic Church. As discussed in Chapter 5, churches had become the sites of massacres rather than sanctuaries of refuge. Not only did people feel betrayed by the lack of assistance by the churches when it was needed most, but questions of a possible complicity of the churches (Rittner, Roth, and Whitworth 2004) remain unanswered until this day.

RELIGION: A MAJOR PLAYER IN CONFLICT RESOLUTION AND RECONCILIATION

Despite these changes, religion remains a major factor in Rwanda's current civil society. While the religious microlevel has undergone major changes, the macrolevel remained nearly the same with still about 90 percent of the population adhering to the Christian faith. Contrary to many secularized countries in the West, religious actors at both the individual and institutionalized levels are significant players in this country's processes of social change: "Religion has been and continues to be part of Rwanda's system of meaning-making and meaning-interpretation, and hence has contributed to shaping new values, demands of propriety and interpretations of old norms that have emerged after the genocide" (Kubai 2016: 3). This holds especially true for Rwanda's process of reconciliation and its quest for sustainable peace and social cohesion. Reconciliation is understood both as a process of healing relationships and as the result of this process. The process includes different elements, such as confessing one's guilt, asking and granting of forgiveness, and making amends. Against the background of the genocide, reconciliation, social unity, and development are explicit topics on the agendas of many churches. The churches generally support the government's top-down reconciliation strategies, yet at the same time they supplement them with bottom-up strategies.

CHRISTIAN CHURCHES IN CONFLICT RESOLUTION AND RECONCILIATION: CONTRIBUTIONS

Based on our discussion of the specific characteristics of religious actors in Chapter 7, the following examines the contributions of Christian churches in Rwanda's reconciliation process. I will make use of the examples of different Church denominations, including "traditional" churches, such as the Presbyterian Church, the Anglican Church, and the Catholic Church, "new" churches, such as Pentecostal Church of Rwanda (ADEPR) and Christian Life Assembly in Kigali, as well as non-church-based Christian actors like Christian Action for Reconciliation and Social Assistance (CARSA). My analysis is based on both literature analysis and recurrent empirical research and ethnographic work I have conducted in Rwanda since 2014.

TRUST: RELIGION AS COMMUNITY, RELIGION AS PRACTICE

Trust in the churches and their moral credibility had been seriously harmed through the genocide. The consequences of the perceived failures of the churches are visible in the changed religious landscape as people turned their backs on the established churches. Regaining the trust of the people thus proved to be a key challenge for many churches as they sought for ways of dealing with the past. While many chose to downplay their actions and inactions during the genocide, some took a different route. A group that included representatives of Tutsi, Hutu, and the West from different church denominations gathered in Detmold, Germany, in 1996 to draft a confession of guilt, the so-called "Detmold Confession". The Confession begins by acknowledging that reconciliation starts with recognizing the suffering of the other and with asking for forgiveness, "The Rwandan people will never be reconciled with each other unless each party accepts to kneel down before the suffering of the other party, to confess their own offense and to humbly ask forgiveness of their victims" (Detmold Confession, §1). For 20 years, the Detmold Confession remained the only one of its kind, until in 2016 the Catholic Church in Rwanda issued a long-awaited apology, followed by a statement of Pope Francis in 2017. Trust needs authenticity, not least in terms of dealing with the past. A genuine confession of guilt helps prepare the ground for sustainable peacebuilding and reconciliation. At the same time, confessions of guilt, apologies, and asking for forgiveness in words, symbols, and deeds are not limited to religious actors, such as churches, but have proven powerful tools of conflict resolution in the political realm as well (cf. The 1970 Warsaw Genuflection of the German chancellor Willy Brandt).

RELATIONSHIPS AND IDENTITY: RELIGION AS COMMUNITY

Many Rwandan churches emphasize the importance of building relationships, of creating a sense of belonging and identity. In the context of the nation's reconciliation process this not only means building relationships with survivors and with perpetrators, but also assisting both in building relationships with one another. Pascal Bataringaya, current President of the Presbyterian Church, sees relationship building as a specific strength of the churches as compared to government initiatives: "The churches have something special. They walk with the people, with the perpetrators, with the victims. People feel that they are not alone" (Bataringaya, Kigali, February 21, 2016, personal interview). Against the background of *ubuntu*, that is, the idea that one's own identity is bound up with that of the other person—"I am because we are" (Tutu 2011), I will illustrate the emphasis on relationships by referring to the example of Remera, a small village in Western Rwanda.

In Remera, the pastor, a trained mediator, of the local Presbyterian congregation founded the "Lights". It is the aim of this group, named after the Gospel of Matthew 5:14 ("You are the light of the world"), to reach out and establish relationships with survivors and perpetrators. Once these relationships are established, they invite both to participate in the weekly meetings of the Lights. During these meetings Christian concepts such as forgiveness, healing, and transformation are discussed, supplemented by insights from trauma therapy, conflict resolution, and mediation. Through the ongoing engagement of the Lights, relationships between survivors and perpetrators are established and supported. The example of Remera illustrates our discussion of social network theory above (Chapter 4.1). It is by means of "connectors"—such as the pastor and the members of the Lights—that different groups and individuals are linked, even across (former) enemy lines. By connecting them, new ideas and concepts, such as on forgiveness or dealing with trauma, are disseminated; a prerequisite for the paradigm change required by complex social processes such as reconciliation and building a new nation.

NETWORKS AND FUNDING: RELIGION AS AN INSTITUTION, RELIGION AS SPIRITUALITY

"Global networking is an inherent characteristic of the whole enterprise of the new churches in Rwanda" (Kubai 2007: 208). The link between local congregations and global partners is visible as churches bring together locals, returnees, and sponsors from abroad. This holds true for both new and traditional churches such as the Presbyterian and the Anglican Church. Their close ties with the German United Evangelical Mission (UEM), for example, facilitate not only networks and connections, but also funding. In terms of conflict resolution, the local-global perspective of many churches can be an asset as resources and knowledge, as well as experiences and best practices are being exchanged across borders. The experiences of Remera, for instance, have attracted interest in places like Germany, the US, Nigeria, or Kenya.

SERVICES: RELIGION AS PRACTICE

As in many other African contexts, the churches in Rwanda pro-vide a number of community services, including education, med-ical services, orphanages, or microfinance. In that way, they do not differ significantly from non-religious actors such as NGOs. Some churches prioritize certain services, while others display a wider array. The Pentecostal Church of Rwanda (ADEPR), for example, focuses on education. With about two million members it self-describes as a "religious organization with the vision consisting of quantitative and qualitative transformation of the Rwandan Community by Jesus Christ Integral Gospel" (Kwizera 2015). ADEPR is responsible for 80 nursery schools, 158 primary schools, 58 secondary schools, six voca-tional and technical schools, and four bible schools. ADEPR's literacy programs throughout the country were awarded prizes by UNESCO. In the post-genocide context of Rwanda, the significance of educa-tion for processes of conflict resolution and peacebuilding can hardly be overemphasized. "Education has played a great role during the rec-onciliation process since it has been used to sensitize the Rwandese society to build the skill of living with diversity" (Sundqvist 2011: 183).

NORMATIVE CONCEPTS AND VALUES: RELIGION AS A SET OF TEACHINGS, RELIGION AS PRACTICE

As people go to church each Sunday, they listen to teachings on dogmatics (what to believe) and ethics (how to behave). As any religion, the Christian faith includes strong normative concepts and values. In the aftermath of the genocide, concepts such as reconcili-ation, forgiveness, and grace have become particularly significant. These theological concepts become very concrete once they are set in the context of torn social fabric and the quest for the healing of broken relationships. Genocide survivor Fr. Marcel Uwineza, S.J, recounts his mixed emotions when he met one of the murderers of his parents, brothers, and sister.

> I thought he was coming to kill me too. But I could not believe what happened. As if in a movie, he knelt before me and asked me to forgive him. After a time of confusion, asking myself what was happening, and by which force I could not describe, I took him, embraced him and said: "I forgive you; the Lord has been good to me." Ever since that

> moment, I have felt free. I have realized that forgiveness heals the for-
> giver even more than the forgiven.
>
> (Uwineza 2016a)

Uwineza's description of "a school of forgiveness" that he perceives God has led him through since the murder of his family is that of a very personal experience, yet it is not an uncommon account, either. Narratives like Uwineza's help illustrate the potency of concepts like forgiveness and healing in transforming attitudes and behaviors.

HOLISTIC PERSPECTIVE: RELIGION AS SPIRITUALITY, RELIGION AS DISCOURSE

Part of Christian theology is a specific understanding of anthro-pology or human nature. Human flourishing is cast not only in terms of physical and material well-being, but also in spiritual and emotional terms. From this holistic understanding follows for many Christian churches that care for the soul must be accompanied by care for the body. Reconciliation initiatives by the churches in Rwanda are therefore often linked to development projects. As Nathan Gasatura, bishop of the Anglican Church, explains,

> The aim is not only to reconcile, but to do projects together, they give them cows together, to feed together, milk the cow together, share the milk together, sell what remains of the milk together, divide the cash together. They would get medical insurances together, build their homes together ... get into cooperatives together, maybe it is rice, maybe it is bee hives, maybe about credit and savings. They also go to church together, celebrate together.
>
> (Gasatura, Butare, February 23, 2016, personal interview)

Connecting the spiritual with the material, and reconciliation with development, the sustainability of both are enhanced as welcome synergies are reaped.

DEALING WITH TRAUMA AND RESTORING MEANING: RELIGION AS A SET OF TEACHINGS, RELIGION AS SPIRITUALITY, RELIGION AS PRACTICE

Violent conflict leaves visible and invisible wounds. If the latter are not treated, they might not only result in severe post-traumatic stress disorder (PTSD), keeping the individual from effectively managing his or her own life. They can also contribute to the spiral of violence that turns former victims into perpetrators. Meanwhile, a quarter of a century after the genocide, second-generation trauma has become a major challenge as the challenges of survivor guilt and finding meaning are being reframed in the next generation. Through developing trust, personal relationships, and feelings of belonging, Christian churches help create a place where trauma can be addressed and healing processes begin, oftentimes by enlisting the help of trained trauma counselors. Trauma healing workshops such as offered by CARSA teach participants strategies to alleviate the effects of PTSD and build resilience (cf. CARSA Trauma Healing). Participants learn to share their stories in a safe way that does not result in re-traumatization and given the opportunity to do so. They furthermore receive counseling in order to give and receive forgiveness. Situating one's own story in the larger eschatological framework of Christian hope can help restore meaning to first and second-generation victims of trauma.

RITUALS: RELIGION AS SPIRITUALITY, RELIGION AS PRACTICE

Rituals provide structure and stability in daily life. Religious rituals, such as prayer, meditation, or communion can become important resources of support, especially in times of social upheaval. Catholic communities in post-genocide Rwanda have attempted to utilize Christian ritual in terms of reconciliation such as in *gacaca nkirisitu* (Christian gacaca), a pastoral process for perpetrators and survivors. Genocide perpetrators are asked to abstain from the sacraments for six months, while participating in a weekly catechetical program. They are encouraged to confront their shame and seek forgiveness from the victims. If both consent, survivors join perpetrators in receiving the Sacrament of Reconciliation. "Echoing ancient church penitential traditions, the priest … performed a ritual rite of reincorporation including the sprinkling of baptismal water" (Carney 2015: 20), followed by a celebratory feast with the entire community. Based on the conviction that reconciliation is a long-term process, the church then assists in facilitating day-to-day relationships between the perpetrator and the survivor.

MEMORY: RELIGION AS A SET OF TEACHINGS, RELIGION AS SPIRITUALITY, RELIGION AS PRACTICE

Memory is central to human identity—to who we are and how we have become who we are. Oftentimes, memory is used to foster hatred and perpetuate stereotypes. Recognizing the importance of memory for reconciliation and sustainable peace, the Christian churches in Rwanda seek to contribute to the healing of memories, for instance, through trauma workshops and their emphasis on forgiveness. Christian churches participate in the nation-wide rituals of remembrance, for instance, through the joint preparation of the week of remembrance following April 7 as the Genocide Memorial Day. At the same time, churches develop their own rituals of commemoration. The Presbyterian congregation in Remera, for instance, erected a memorial site with the names and graves of the church members killed at a prominent place next to the church. There, survivors have a place for their grief as their murdered loved ones are being acknowledged by the community. Bringing Christian eschatological hope and a framework that reaches beyond the individual lifespan to people's despair is the "theological imperative of memory" in post-genocide Rwanda (Uwinzea 2016b).

CHRISTIAN CHURCHES IN CONFLICT RESOLUTION AND RECONCILIATION: CHALLENGES

Next to the significant contributions of the Christian churches and their potentials for supporting, if not leading positive social change, the following problems emerge.

REINVENTING SOCIAL CLEAVAGES

Rwanda's reconciliation process is marked by the official motto "We are all Rwandan". Much political and social energy has been invested in the creation of one collective national identity, transcending former ethnic identities. Yet the problem seems to be more complex as additional layers of identity are being added to society, for instance, by returnees from Anglophone and Francophone countries. These emerging new social alignments are also visible in some churches as language, common backgrounds, and affluency become markers of identity. For example, Christian Life Assembly, one of the fastest growing churches in Kigali, represents an Anglophone identity, with many members being returnees from East Africa. The apparent affluence of its members is a further identity marker of this church. Especially in urban contexts it seems, therefore, as if "the churches have wittingly or unwittingly reinvented new layers of identity" (Kubai 2007: 212), thereby inadvertently countering their own reconciliation efforts.

LACK OF ATTENTION TO HUMAN RIGHTS

For years, Rwanda has been criticized for its tight political control, state intimidation, and suppression of basic human rights (Human Rights Watch 2019: 491–495). One example is the problematic situation of the Twa people, a minority of about 1 percent. Traditionally hunters and gatherers, the Twa have suffered political and social marginalization for decades. In April 2016, the UN Committee on the Elimination of Racial Discrimination issued an official warning that the Twa are threatened by extinction. Yet within Rwanda's current political discourse on national unity that obliterates different social groups, the problem of the Twa cannot even be adequately framed. The denial of ethnic plurality results, in this case, in the denial of basic human rights to a certain group of people, with harmful consequences to the nation's process of social unity and reconciliation. Perhaps due to the harsh political climate, the churches have so far expressed little interest in issues of human rights, thereby neglecting their role as advocates on behalf of the poor and marginalized.

(TOO) CLOSE CHURCH AND STATE RELATIONSHIP

In general, Christian churches in Rwanda seek good relationships with the state. In terms of conflict resolution and reconciliation, the churches support the state-led top-down initiatives. Quantitative studies support our findings here that there are no systematic differences between the different religious groups and their engagement in peacebuilding (Bazuin 2013). The close relationship between the churches and the state is illustrated by the presence of (former) church representatives in higher government positions, such as the president of the "National Unity and Reconciliation Commission" (NURC), an Anglican bishop. The reconciliation and forgiveness rhetoric of the state aligns well with the churches' own core values. At the same time, the churches mostly abstain from critically addressing problematic state conduct. This lack of prophetic stance has evoked some inner-church criticism (Kazuyuki 2009; Nsengimana 2015), yet mostly the churches "try to see how to gain favor from the state instead of challenging it" (Nsengimana 2015: 108).

ONE-SIDED CONCEPT OF RECONCILIATION

Processes of reconciliation must pay adequate attention to peace, justice, mercy, and truth in order to be sustainable (Lederach 1999). Yet in the context of the Rwandan reconciliation process, churches seem to focus primarily on mercy and peace, while neglecting justice and truth. This impression is supported by Josephine Sundqvist's study on Pentecostal churches and reconciliation. "The Pentecostal movement has barely been emphasizing justice in their reconciliation strategy or their interpretation of the concept" (Sundqvist 2011: 169). The neglect of justice and truth is visible, for instance, in a problematic official discourse on memory that primarily enforces the "narrative of the victor", while suppressing dissenting voices. If reconciliation lacks justice and truth, however, resentment towards it is likely to build up.

CONCLUSION

A thorough understanding of post-genocide Rwanda's ongoing major social experiment called "Politics of Reconciliation" needs to take the contributions of religious actors into account. Churches successfully contribute to the social change needed for sustainable peace on multiple levels. Their specific contributions display both formal and material characteristics. Formal aspects such as building trust and personal relationships with survivors and perpetrators or offering different community services such as health care and education are supplemented by material aspects such as disseminating normative concepts and values related to reconciliation and forgiveness, while offering meaning and hope in the face of a traumatic past. At the same time, certain challenges emerge. A one-sided understanding of reconciliation neglecting justice, a Church–state relationship lacking critical distance, and a lack of explicit concern regarding the state's human rights violations seem to be amongst the most pertinent problematic aspects threatening to turn "thick" and substantial reconciliation into a "thin" and formal process.

REFERENCES

Amman, Daniel. (2015). "A Country of Hope: Africa. Rise of a Continent", *Credit Suisse Bulletin*, 3: 30–45.

Bazuin, Joshua T. (2013). "Religion in the Remaking of Rwanda After Genocide", Ph.D. Dissertation, Vanderbilt University.

Bouka, Y. (2018). "Rwanda", in Jon Abbink, V. Adetula, A. Mehler, and H. Melber (eds.), *Africa Yearbook Volume 14. Politics, Economy and Society South of the Sahara in 2017*. Leiden: Boston, 342–352.

Carney, J.J. (2015). "A Generation After Genocide: Catholic Reconciliation in Rwanda", *Theological Studies*, 76(4): 785–812.

Christian Action for Reconciliation and Social Assistance (CARSA). "Trauma Healing & Reconciliation". Viewed from: www.carsaministry.org/trauma-healing-reconciliation/ [Date accessed October 31, 2019].

Dallaire, Roméo. (2004). *Shake Hands with the Devil. The Failure of Humanity in Rwanda*. London: Da Capo Press.

Detmold Confession. (1996). Viewed from www.rwandahope.com/confession.pdf [Date accessed November 1, 2019].

Human Rights Watch. (2019). *World Report 2019*. Viewed from www.hrw.org/de/world-report/2019 [Date accessed October 31, 2019].

Kazuyuki, Sasaki. (2009). "Beyond Dichotomies. The Quest for Justice and Reconciliation and the Politics of National Identity Building in Post-Genocide Rwanda", Ph.D. Dissertation, Bradford.

Kubai, Anne. (2007). "Post-Genocide Rwanda: The Changing Religious Landscape", *Exchange*, 36: 198–214.

Kubai, Anne. (2016). "'Confession' and 'Forgiveness' as a Strategy for Development in Post-Genocide Rwanda", *HTS Teologiese Studies / Theological Studies*, 42(4): 1–9.

Kwizera, Emmanuel. (2015). "ADEPR Education Ministry". *Pentecostal Church in Rwanda ADEPR*. Viewed from: www.en.adepr.rw/spip.php?article61 [Date accessed October 31, 2019].

Lederach, John P. (1999). "'Justpeace.' in European Centre for Conflict Prevention", *People Building Peace*, Utrecht: European Centre for Conflict Prevention, 27–36.

National Institute of Statistics of Rwanda. (2014). *Socio-Cultural Characteristics of the Population*. Viewed from: www.statistics.gov.rw/publication/rphc4-thematic-report-socio-cultural-characteristics-population [Date accessed October 31, 2019].

Nsengimana, Célestin. (2015). *Peacebuilding Initiatives of the Presbyterian Church in Post-Genocide Rwandan Society. An Impact Assessment*. Geneva: Globethics.net.

Rittner, Carole, Roth, John K., and Whitworth, Wendy (eds.). (2004). *Genocide in Rwanda. Complicity of the Churches?* St Paul, MN: Paragon House.

Sundqvist, Josephine. (2011). "Reconciliation as a Societal Process. A Case Study on the Role of the Pentecostal Movement (ADEPR) as an Actor in the Reconciliation Process in Post-Genocide Rwanda", *Svensk Missionstidsskrift*, 99: 157–195.

Tutu, Desmond. (2011). *God Is Not a Christian: And Other Provocations*. New York: HarperOne.

Uwineza, Marcel. (2016a). "On Christian Hope", *America. The Jesuit Review*, April, 4–11. Viewed from: www.americamagazine.org/issue/christian-hope [Date accessed October 31, 2019].

Uwineza, Marcel. (2016b). "Memory: A Theological Imperative in Post-Genocide Rwanda", *Hekima Review*, 54: 51–65.

10

ISLAMIC PERSPECTIVE
RELIGION IN MUSLIM WOMEN'S PEACEBUILDING INITIATIVES IN PAKISTAN

S. Ayse Kadayifci-Orellana

INTRODUCTION

Militant groups, in the name of Islam, continue to threaten peace and security in the Western and Muslim worlds. Pakistan is one of the countries that suffers most from the attacks of these groups. For instance, in December 2014, gunmen stormed the Army Public School in Peshawar, setting off explosives and firing automatic weapons, killing more than 148, mostly children. The Tehreek-e Taliban Pakistan claimed responsibility for the attack. Within this context, Mossarat Qadeem, a Muslim woman in Pakistan, founded the PAIMAN Alumni Trust (PAIMAN), a national organization working at the grassroots level, to address radicalization and extremist violence, and also to build peace in the conflict-ridden regions of the Federally Administered Tribal Areas (FATA) of Pakistan and Khyber Pakhtunkhwa (KP). Based on the principle of "local ownership", PAIMAN draws its conflict resolution from Islamic and Pakistani traditions and values. This case study will explore how PAIMAN, empowered by Islam, works to address extremist violence in Pakistan. It considers: (1) religion as a community, which explores how Muslim identity provides women with credibility and legitimacy to resolve conflicts and build peace; (2) religion as practice, which examines how PAIMAN assists women and youth impacted by violence and conflict in Pakistan by engaging and supported them, and (3) religion as a set of teachings, which describes how Islamic values inform their work.

RELIGION, CONFLICT RESOLUTION, AND PEACEBUILDING

Since 9/11 the role of religion in conflict has become a main area of interest. In order to respond to religiously motivated conflicts, scholars and practitioners have pointed out that our policies must be based on a deeper understanding of the dynamics of religion, violence, and conflict resolution, and must address the unique needs and opportunities of the communities within their religio-cultural contexts. Consequently, the potential of religious traditions as sources of peace and the crucial role religious actors can play are increasingly being recognized by governmental agencies as well as non-governmental organizations working in the field of security, conflict resolution, and peacebuilding. This recognition has led institutions such as USAID (2019), the World Bank (2015), and the United Nations (UNIATF 2018) to identify engagement with religion and faith-based actors as an important component of the 2030 Sustainable Development Goals (SDGs).

Religious peacebuilding includes a range of activities performed by religious actors or religiously motivated individuals and groups for the purpose of resolving and transforming conflict and building sustainable peace. Engaging in religious peacebuilding can provide a spiritual basis for transformation and supplement the mechanistic and instrumental conflict resolution models. Religion can bring social, moral, and spiritual resources to the peacebuilding process. They can also inspire a sense of engagement and commitment to resolving conflict and to transforming conflictual relationships into peaceful ones, especially because religion incorporate ideals of peace. Furthermore, they provide vocabulary, images, and myths exemplars to serve as symbols and models of peace, as well as a range of values and principles to guide conflict resolution. Religious involvement in peacemaking initiatives can prepare and equip conflict resolution practitioners and diplomats for proactive roles in transforming the conflict. As Abu-Nimer (2001: 686) notes, "Framing the interventions within a religious context and deriving tools from a religious narrative have made it possible for interveners to gain access and increase their potential impact on the parties". Gopin (2000: 15) supports this by stating that

> a close study of the sacred texts, traditions, symbols and myths that emerge in conflict situations may contribute to theoretical approaches to conflict analysis by providing a useful frame of reference for conflict resolution workshops, and interfaith dialogue groups, and by creating a bridge to the unique cultural expression of a particular conflict.

Religious peacebuilding, then, could become a major tool for training, empowering, and motivating religiously oriented people towards peace.

WHERE ARE THE WOMEN IN FAITH-BASED ACTORS?

Engaging religious actors and developing intervention strategies have been incorporated to address Islamic militancy in Pakistan. Noticing that religious actors have more credibility and legitimacy than secular actors, governmental organizations such as USAID, OECD, and the Interior Ministries of Iraq and Pakistan have started to work with religious leaders and develop counter-narrative strategies that aim to deconstruct, discredit, or demystify groups like Taliban and al-Qaeda and to de-radicalize or disengage their followers (Briggs and Feve 2013). However, these approaches focused on traditional religious leaders, which are often men, and have rarely recognized the important role women have been playing in responding to violence and building peace in their communities. Gendered approaches to peace and security are mainly articulated by the Women, Peace and Security (WPS) community which emphasizes addressing women's needs and empowering them at times of conflict, mostly through secular approaches. Much of the research and discussions still presume religious women are voiceless victims of religion and religious institutions and therefore are in need of being saved. Hence, the important work Muslim women activists are doing in their communities to respond to violent extremism and their intervention strategies rooted in Islamic theology go unnoticed.

It is often the case that, in many religious traditions, women's role in the public sphere is limited as a result of patriarchal interpretation of religious text, and many male religious actors ignore or obstruct women's leadership in peacebuilding and conflict resolution efforts (Hayward and Marshall 2015: 13). Muslim women, in particular, have often been perceived as victims of not only violence committed by militant organizations but by Islam in general. Hence, emancipation and empowerment of Muslim women have been an integral part of foreign policy objectives and democratization, and development efforts by many Western governments and organizations. While it is true that Muslim women are often victims of patriarchal structures and discriminatory practices, this depiction of Muslim women as victims does not tell the whole story. Many Muslim women are inspired by their faith and believe Islam calls for justice and peacebuilding. They are increasingly playing critical peacebuilding roles either by organizing to stop violence and end the conflict or developing initiatives.

PAIMAN AND ISLAMIC SOURCES OF CONFLICT RESOLUTION

One such example of a Muslim woman working on building peace in her community is Mossarat Qadeem, who co-founded PAIMAN, a non-profit organization in 2004 (www.paimantrust.org). Within an Islamic framework, PAIMAN works directly with youth as well as mothers of radicalized youth, female community leaders, teachers, and elected representatives to respond to violent extremism and build resiliency in her community in Khyber Pakhtunkhwa (KP) and the Federally Administered Tribal Areas (FATA) of Pakistan (Peace Direct 2019). Based on the belief that there is an urgent need for developing the understanding of people on various aspects of conflict transformation and peacebuilding and its application at a community level, PAIMAN aims to neutralize extremist tendencies through community mobilization, active citizenship, and community empowerment for building social cohesion (ICAN 2017). To accomplish this, PAIMAN established the Center for Conflict Transformation and Peacebuilding in Islamabad to act as a resource center and training institute in South Asia. Initiatives of PAIMAN engage various local actors such as elected officials, youth, women madrasa teachers, religious leaders, and journalists, amongst others, from conflict-affected areas. PAIMAN also trains women, particularly mothers, and youth in a number of different areas to increase local capacity for addressing violent extremism. Recognizing "[A] woman's role is not just a mother, but also an activist, a teacher, a religious scholar, a political leader, a decision maker, and a peace negotiator" (ICAN 2017). Qadeem's organization has trained 14,000 males and females, who then became members of Peace groups called TOLANA to promote peace and counter violent extremism within the community (ICAN 2017). Amongst other tasks, they use social media, and hold community sessions at schools, madrasas, and public places to create awareness and to discuss how to address extremism. The PAIMAN Alumni Trust also developed an inclusive peace curriculum and trained 220 teachers of private schools and 98 teachers of madrassas who then use the curriculum in their respective schools and madrassas.

MUSLIM IDENTITY AS A SOURCE OF CREDIBILITY AND LEGITIMACY: RELIGION AS COMMUNITY

Muslim women who are working in their communities to respond to violence and build peace, like Qadeem, frame their efforts within their Muslim identity and the religio-cultural traditions of Islam. Despite all the challenges faced by Muslim women peacebuilders, they are often inspired and empowered by Islam to work towards peace. Given that Islam is the primary source of legitimacy in Muslim communities, the women's religious identity and their efforts to use Islamic texts, images, concepts, and vocabulary provides them with legitimacy and credibility that is vital to the success of peacebuilding actors. More particularly, when the conflict and violence is framed within a religious framework, as is the case with the Taliban and al-Qaeda, it becomes even more important to frame the responses to it within the same religious framework. Therefore, to be considered legitimate and authentic, the women derive their conflict resolution and peacebuilding approaches from the Quran, hadith, and sunna.

Islam and their Muslim identity were an important source of legitimacy for PAIMAN and Qadeem in reaching out to youth, women, and religious leaders in their community. One of the strategies of PAIMAN was to build women's capacity for critical thinking, allowing them to recognize indicators of violent extremism in an individual and in their communities, and to find ways to address these early warning signs by promoting dialogue and community peacebuilding. This required them to find ways to make women aware of their potential in influencing and guiding their children's lives, and in preventing them from engaging in extremist activities. Because, in almost all cases, the extremists used the text of the Quran to attract youth and communities towards the concept of violent jihad, the women needed to develop a strategy that was rooted in the Islamic discourse. This was important particularly for them to gain legitimacy to offer narratives countering the extremist interpretations. Therefore, PAIMAN based their initiatives within an Islamic framework, used the Quranic verses and the *Sunna* to reach out to radicalized and vulnerable youth, and to help transform the mindset of these mothers. For, instance, regarding their work with mothers, Qadeem notes, their "transformative methodology is based on the Quran and Sunnah, as Prophet Muhammad (PBUH) insists that a mother's role is vital in the upbringing of her children in accordance with the values of true Islamic teaching, which does not preach hatred or violence" (Qadeem 2018: 8). Consequently, PAIMAN was able to offer an alternative understanding of jihad and justice.

SERVICE FOR WOMEN IMPACTED BY CONFLICT: RELIGION AS PRACTICE

Often inspired by their faith, many religious actors provide a number of different services in their communities, ranging from providing food, clean water, or education, amongst other amenities. During conflicts, the religious actors may also provide services to help resolve conflict and build relationships between the parties. Conflicts and violence impact men and women in various ways and they have different needs and opportunities. In conservative communities, where interactions between men and women are restricted, women can work with female victims and perpetrators of violence more easily, and have resources that may not be available to male religious leaders, as it is the case with PAIMAN in Pakistan. Associated with the honor of the family and the community, their contact with outsiders, especially men, is often constrained. Stigma associated with secular women's organizations also limits their access to more conservative women in these communities. Since advancing women's status and rights is an important dimension of peacebuilding, development, and countering violent extremism, it is particularly critical for women who have a good understanding of other women's needs and concerns, and who have legitimacy to work with them, to reach out to women who have been impacted by violence.

Many Muslim women work on a number of issues engaging different actors in their communities. One of the areas Muslim women are uniquely positioned to work is addressing the impact of conflict on women and children. Conflict in Pakistan put additional burdens on women there. Imposing a strict gender code based on their interpretation of Islam, extremist groups limited women's and girls' mobility and participation in social and cultural life, such as going outside of the home without a male escort and participation in social and political activities. Women were excluded from working in public and private sectors. Qadeem states that those women and girls who failed to comply with this interpretation of Islam were often subjected to harsh punitive measures for defying the social practices (Qadeem 2018: 4–5). In addition to being physically attacked by these groups, more than 400 girls' schools in the Swat region were destroyed and burned and many girls were prevented from attending the schools that remained (Qadeem 2018: 4). Fear of punishment even prevented many of the female health workers and doctors from providing basic health care to women. As Qadeem puts it, extremists were engaged in "gender apartheid, but nobody dared to raise a voice against them" (Qadeem 2018: 5) because anybody who would talk about women's rights was ostracized for being anti-Islamic and pro-west.

In addition to being victims of violence, some women in Pakistan had become supporters of militant organizations and their jihadi ideology. Qadeem (2018: 8) states that women were easily influenced by the jihadi sermons of extremist leaders whose notion of jihad transcended gender, and who used a convergence of propaganda, media attention, and intellectual and theological ignorance to construct a hybrid role for women in their idea of an Islamic society. Some of the mothers also wanted to provide support for their sons who were involved in extremist groups. PAIMAN also found that as a result of socially accepted gender roles women often followed the instructions and advice of their male relatives. Within this context, working with women was particularly important.

Recognizing that engaging women in general, and mothers in particular, was critical to counter extremist violence in Pakistan, PAIMAN developed an integrated approach to empower women socially, economically, and psychologically. This multilayered approach focused on building women's capacity in critical thinking, dialogue, and community peacebuilding, to help them recognize early signs of extremism in order to prevent them and to make them aware of their potential in influencing and guiding their children's lives. Moreover, PAIMAN sought to provide them with livelihood skills, thereby raising their status and voice in their families and communities and reducing their vulnerability to violent extremism. PAIMAN also worked to build the capacity of female school and madrassa teachers, police women, and female leaders of religious political parties and activists, and to form a coalition known as "Women of faith building social cohesion in Pakistan" (Qadeem 2018: 7). Finally, PAIMAN also provided education to women on Islamic teachings and texts that promote tolerance and gender equality and helped women to understand their role in promoting a culture of tolerance and peace and encouraging resilient communities. PAIMAN's trainings also focused on building self-confidence, competences, and basic skills in understanding attitudinal and behavioral changes in their sons. For example, PAIMAN, to this date has trained more than 235 female teachers, including those from religious schools in their peace curriculum that emphasizes values of pluralism and harmony, and reached more than 6,400 students (Qadeem 2018: 11).

Following these trainings, participants became members of PAIMAN mothers' peace groups called Mothers Tolana ("together" in Pashto) (Qadeem 2016). Through the 23 Mothers Tolana (with a total of 1,500 members), PAIMAN has reached out to 23,198 women and worked to reintegrate 1,450 extremist and vulnerable youth through a phased process that includes psycho-social counseling (Qadeem 2018: 9). Mothers Tolana hold community meetings with other women and have been instrumental in identifying vulnerable and extremist youth and mothers who support them. Qadeem explains that when the Mothers Tolana found

out that 30 women were supporting extremism by stitching suicide bomber jackets, they met with them to talk to them. When,
during their conversation, the woman who supplies the jackets to
the extremists was asked whether she knew what they were used for,
she explained to them:

> Of course I know, we are all engaged in a jihad. I haven't told the other
> women who sew the jackets, but they must know. What other use can
> these strange jackets be for? I know whom I am supplying, I know
> what they are being used for and I am putting my bit in the jihad that is
> being carried out against the infidels.

(ICAN 2018)

The woman also explained, in addition to contributing to jihad,
stitching these jackets brought them respect and security, and
provided with an income as they were paid to do so. Through
their efforts, the Tolana Mothers and Qadeem provided the women
with alternative sources of livelihood by helping them make dresses
instead, and explaining "that going to heaven can be done in many
other ways, without the need to be part of a group that kills people"
(ICAN 2018). They were able to convince 13 of the 30 women
involved in the stitching of suicide bombing jackets to stop.

ISLAMIC VALUES OF PEACE AND CONFLICT RESOLUTION: RELIGION AS A SET OF TEACHINGS

Islamic values and principles play an important role in Muslim
women's efforts (Kadayifci-Orellana 2015: 196–201) because as "a
powerful constituent of cultural norms" they influence individual
and social conceptions of peace and conflict, including jihad. For
this reason, extremist groups in Pakistan base their ideology within
Islamic frameworks and use religious texts selectively and out of
context, especially regarding jihad, to recruit followers (ICAN
2018). They exploit the fact that most Pakistanis do not speak
Arabic and many Pakistanis depend on the interpretation of religious leaders. However, Islam tradition is replete with teachings
and practices of nonviolence and peace (Kadayifci-Orellana, Abu-
Nimer, and Saleem 2013). Muslims often point out that Islam itself
is derived from the word *slm*, which means peace and safety. There
are many references to peace (*salam, silm, sulh*, etc.) in the Quran that

indicate that peace, together with justice (*adl*), is a central message of Islam (Q3:83; 4:58; 5:8; 10:25; 16:90; 41:11; 42:15; 57:25). Based on these verses, peace in Islam is associated with a wide range of values and principles of peace such as *Tawhid* (unity of God), *Fitrah* (original constitution of human beings as good), *Khilafah* (humans as vicegerents of God on earth), *Adl* (justice), *Rahmah* and *Rahim* (compassion and mercy), *Afu* (forgiveness), *Sabr* (patience), and *Hubb* (love) (cf. Kadayifci-Orellana et al. 2013: 8), which urge Muslims to resolve their conflicts peacefully. These values and principles can provide a moral framework, inform attitudes, and guide action towards resolving conflicts. Islamic sources lay down fundamental Islamic ethical principles and moral values to provide guidance and coherence to Muslim conflict resolution practices across cultures and historical periods. Many of these continue to inspire Muslim peacemakers in their efforts to establish a just and sustainable peace.

As Abu-Nimer (2003: 71) states, "Peacebuilding in Islam is based on a framework of deeply embedded religious beliefs regarding individuals' responsibility for their actions and their active participation in larger social contexts". The Quran constantly reminds Muslims about the value of justice, which is a divine command, and not an option, therefore it is the responsibility of all Muslims to work towards the establishment of justice, including social and economic justice, for all (Q4:135; 57:25; 5:8; 2:178; 2:30; 16:90). The Quranic notion of justice is universal and valid for all human beings with the universality of justice being clearly expressed in the following Quranic verses: "O ye who believe! Stand out firmly for justice as witnesses to Allah even as against yourselves, your parents or your kin, and whether it be (against) the rich and poor' (Q4:135) or "To fair dealing, and let not the hatred of others to you make you swerve to wrong and depart from justice. Be just for it is next to Piety" (Q5:8). Therefore, the Qur'an calls Muslims to mobilize and act against injustice, even if a Muslim originates the injustice (Q4:135). The universality of justice for all, not only for Muslims, is critical for the resolution of conflicts and developing peaceful relations.

Because of the critical role religious teachings play in the justification of jihad, PAIMAN has developed a counter-narrative based on Quranic teachings and Islamic values of peace. As Qadeem (2016) states:

> In almost all cases the extremists used the text of the Quran to attract youth and communities towards the concept of violent jihad or convince them to act in an extremist fashion. We used the Quranic verses in their appropriate context to help transform the mindset of these mothers.

In their work with mothers PAIMAN found that women had no weapon to fight against violent extremism because they were unaware of the basic interpretation of the Quran (PAIMAN n.d.: 19). In that respect, Qadeem points out that in their work they employ Islamic values and principles, particularly Quranic texts and hadith. To counter violence and to promote a culture of tolerance and peace PAIMAN uses Islamic teachings and texts. For example, Qadeem states (2018: 8):

> To counter this extremist strategy, it was crucial to educate women on Islamic teachings and texts that promote tolerance and gender equality and help them in understanding their role in promoting a culture of tolerance and peace and encouraging resilient communities.

So, the PAIMAN community sessions have always been grounded in the interpretation of "Peace" and "Jihad in the light of the Holy Quran" and provided Quranic education by engaging *Aalima* (women religious leaders) because women believed that "once they were well versed about the concepts of peace and jihad they would be in a better position to educate their children to prevent them from being radicalized" (PAIMAN n.d.: 20). In addition to the Quranic verses, the prophet's life and dealings with non-Muslims based on tolerance and patience were referred to as examples. As a result, women became more aware of Islamic conceptions of peace and jihad and were able to counter narratives that called for violence (PAIMAN n.d.: 20).

CONCLUSION

Islamic tradition is replete with teachings that promote peace, harmony, and co-existence. The Quran and Prophet's tradition provide Muslims with values, principles, and examples of resolving conflicts and building peace. Responding to extremist violence in the name of Islam requires developing strategies and counter narratives rooted within this tradition. Many Muslim women, like Qadeem and her organization PAIMAN, work in their communities to resolve conflicts and build peace. As this case study illustrated, Islam as a community informs their identity and gives them credibility and legitimacy to work to counter religiously based violent extremism. Islam as practiced can inspire and empower women to develop approaches to work effectively with mothers to prevent radicalization of their children, address gender-based violence, collaborate with imams and religious schools to develop peace-oriented curricula, promote peace and social cohesion, as well as prevent numerous youth from joining extremist groups. Islam as a set of teachings provided the theological framework of their peace work and narratives countering extremists' understanding of jihad.

REFERENCES

Abu-Nimer, Mohammed. (2001). "Conflict Resolution, Culture, and Religion: Toward a Training Model of Interreligious Peacebuilding", *Peace Research,* 38(6): 685–704.

Abu-Nimer, Mohammed. (2003). *Nonviolence and Peacebuilding in Islam.* Florida: University Press of Florida.

Briggs, R. and Feve, S. (2013). "Review of Programs to Counter Narratives of Violent Extremism: What Works and What are the Implications for Government?" *Institute for Strategic Dialogue.* [Online]. Viewed from www. publicsafety.gc.ca/cnt/ntnl-scrt/cntr-trrrsm/r-nd-flght-182/knshk/ctlg/ dtls-en.aspx?i=127 [Date accessed October 10, 2019].

Gopin, Marc. (2000). *Between Eden and Armageddon: The Future of World Religions Violence, and Peacemaking.* New York: Oxford University Press.

Hayward, S. and Marshall, K. (2015). "Religious Women's Invisibility: Obstacles and Opportunities", in Susan Hayward and Katherine Marshall (eds.) *Women, Religion and Peacebuilding: Illuminating the Unseen.* Washington, DC: USIP Press.

International Civil Society Action Network (ICAN). (2017). "Peace Heroes: Pakistani Activist Mossarat Qadeem Responds to Donald Trump" *MS Magazine,* October 31, 2017. [Online]. Viewed from https://msmagazine. com/2017/10/31/peace-heroes-pakistani-activist-mossarat-qadeem- responds-donald-trump/ [Date accessed October 10, 2019].

International Civil Society Action Network (ICAN). (2018). Interview with Mossarat Qadeem by ICAN (January 25, 2018). [Online] "Mossarat Qadeem and Tolana Mothers: Cutting off Extremists' Resources—One Thread at a Time". Viewed from www.icanpeacework.org/2017/10/31/peace-heroes-pakistan-mossarat-qadeem-responds-trump/ [Date accessed October 10, 2019].

International Civil Society Action Network (ICAN) and Rana Allam. (2018). "These Pakistani Women are Cutting Off Extremists' Resources—One Threat at a Time?" *MS Magazine*, January 24, 2018. [Online]. Viewed from https://msmagazine.com/2018/01/24/pakistani-women-cutting-off-extremists-resources-one-thread-time/ [Date accessed October 10, 2019].

Kadayifci-Orellana. S., Ayse. (2015). "Muslim Women Building Peace: Challenges and Opportunities", in Yasmin Sakia and Chad Haines (eds.), *Women and Peace in the Islamic World: Gender, Agency and Influence*. I.B. Tauris & Co Ltd, 191–223.

Kadayifci-Orellana, S., Ayse, Abu-Nimer, M., and Saleem, A.M. (2013). *Understanding an Islamic Framework for Peacebuilding*. Islamic Relief Worldwide, Birmingham. [Online]. Viewed from http://policy.islamic-relief.com/publication/ [Date accessed October 10, 2019].

PAIMAN Trust. (n.d). "PAIMAN TOLANA: The Torch Bearers Countering Violent Extremism Success Stories from the Field". Viewed from http://paimantrust.org/wp-content/uploads/2015/05/Casestudies-EU.pdf [Date accessed October 10, 2019].

Peace Direct. (2019). "PAIMAN Alumni Trust (PAIMAN)". [Online]. Viewed from 28e Oct 4.3. Christian docxhttps://www.peaceinsight.org/conflicts/pakistan/peacebuilding-organisations/paiman-alumni-trust-paiman/ [Date accessed October 10, 2019].

Qadeem, Mossarat. (2016). "Women's Participation in Transforming Conflict and Violent Extremism", *UN Chronicle*, Vol. LII, No. 4, April 2016. [Online]. Viewed from https://unchronicle.un.org/article/womens-participation-transforming-conflict-and-violent-extremism [Date accessed October 10, 2019].

Qadeem, Mossarat. (2018). "Engendering Extremism: Women Preventing and Countering Violent Extremism in Pakistan". LSE Center for Women, Peace and Security. Paper 16/2018. [Online]. Viewed from www.lse.ac.uk/women-peace-security/assets/documents/2018/wps16Qadeem.pdf [Date accessed October 10, 2019].

United Nations InterAgency Task Force (UNIATF). (2018). "Engaging Religion and Faith-based Actors on Agenda 2030/The SDGS 2017". Annual Report of the United Nations Inter-Agency Task Force on Engaging Faith-based Actors for Sustainable Development. United Nations. [Online]. Viewed from www.unaoc.org/wp-content/uploads/Annual-Report-IATF-on-Religion-and-Development-Jan-18.pdf [Date accessed October 10, 2019].

United States Agency for International Development (USAID). (2019). "U.S. Strategy on Religious Leader and Faith Community Engagement". [Online]. Viewed from www.usaid.gov/faith-and-opportunity-initiatives/us-strategy [Date accessed October 10, 2019].

World Bank. (2015). "The World Bank Group's Engagement with Faith-Based and Religious Organizations". [Online]. Viewed from https://jliflc.com/wp/wp-content/uploads/2015/07/Faith-Based-flyer-4-14-15web.pdf [Date accessed October 10, 2019].

PART V
NOW WHAT?

11

NOW WHAT?

IMPLICATIONS FOR ACADEMICS, POLICY MAKERS, AND PRACTITIONERS

Christine Schliesser, S. Ayse Kadayifci-Orellana, and Pauline Kollontai

Our case studies, ranging from ongoing land disputes in Israel to the continuous quest for sustainable peace and reconciliation in post–genocide Rwanda and women responding to violence in their communities in Pakistan, show the significance of religion in each of these conflicts. With different faith traditions in each context, their roles reveal remarkable similarities as religion has been used for both good and bad. How can we then, as academics, policy makers, and practitioners, better understand the concrete role of religion in a given conflict? And how can we strengthen the constructive resources religion brings to conflict resolution? Based on, but at the same time going beyond our discussion, we now present nine concrete implications and recommendations for academics, policy makers and practitioners.

IMPLICATION 1: BRIDGING THE DIVIDE BETWEEN RELIGIOUS AND SECULAR

Religious peacebuilding "still operates on the fringes of the larger field of peace and conflict resolution, which is itself situated on the fringes of international relations, a field dominated by real-politik or a hegemonic power paradigm" (Abu-Nimer 2015: 16). The side-lining happens from two sides. On the one hand, religious peacebuilding is still often ignored by the secular side. Governmental and NGO-based efforts for integration must therefore include promoting religious literacy in government, business, media, and higher education (McDonagh 2018: 26). On the other hand, many religious initiatives are designed and implemented independent of secular efforts. Here, theological reflection that stresses the cooperative and public dimensions of faith can be helpful, for instance, in public theology (Storrar and Morton 2004). Efforts towards integration must happen from both sides.

IMPLICATION 2: BRIDGING THE DIVIDE BETWEEN DIFFERENT FAITH TRADITIONS

Besides the necessity for bridging the religious–secular divide, there is a need for more and deeper cooperation between different faith traditions in conflict resolution. More often than not, ignorance and prejudices hinder interfaith cooperation. Interfaith dialogue and joint initiatives, however, can serve as powerful inspirations for overcoming violence, not only within a particular conflict, but also far beyond it. The example of Imam Muhammad Ashafa and Pastor James Wuye, former enemies who overcame their own enmity, not only helped to re-establish peace and trust in their own warring communities in Nigeria, but the interfaith methodology developed by them has been employed in Africa and beyond (for further examples on interfaith conflict resolution see Abu-Nimer and Augsburger 2009).

IMPLICATION 3: BRIDGING THE DIVIDE BETWEEN ACADEMICS, POLICY MAKERS, AND PRACTITIONERS

Effective conflict resolution depends on the cooperation of all relevant actors, religious or not, including academics, policy makers and practitioners. One powerful example is the "Pathfinders for Peaceful, Just and Inclusive Societies", a joint endeavor by the governments of Brazil, Sierra Leone, and Switzerland to fulfill the vision of SDG 16+ (Peace, Justice, and Strong Institutions). This roadmap aims to "mobilize partners from all sectors behind a shared vision" (Pathfinders 2017: 7), including policy makers from the UN and national governments, religious and secular NGOs, and academics. At the same time, integration here goes beyond its functional dimension in terms of a broad coalition between all relevant partners. Integration also refers to the interconnectedness between SDG 16 and other SDGs. This is signified by the plus in SDG 16+. For peace cannot be viewed in abstraction from education, gender equality, and climate change, to name just three related challenges.

IMPLICATION 4: MORE EVALUATION

Despite the increasing number of programs focusing on religious peacebuilding, there is a knowledge gap in the area of evaluation (Vader 2015) and there is a "pressing need for greater monitoring and evaluation of religious peacebuilding work – and peacebuilding generally" (Hayward 2012: 8). One of the pioneer studies in this area is the meta-review of interreligious peacebuilding evaluations, which was conducted by Peacebuilding Evaluation Consortium (PEC), led by Alliance for Peacebuilding (Vader 2015). Evaluation of religious peacebuilding generates better understanding of what is effective religious peacebuilding, and supports evidence-based policy and practice. A deeper understanding of the nature and impact, as well as strengths and weaknesses of religious conflict resolution, would in turn help with integrating it into the larger academic, political, and societal frameworks.

One helpful example is the South African Reconciliation Barometer, the world's longest running public opinion survey on national reconciliation. Since 2003, the Institute for Justice and Reconciliation (IJR) in South Africa conducts nationally representative public opinion surveys on South Africans' attitudes towards reconciliation. While not specifically geared towards examining the role of religion in reconciliation, its extensive data base allows for the reconstruction of the impact of religion. The availability of all surveys online not only ensures the worldwide accessibility of the data, but also facilitates chronological and comparative approaches necessary for in-depth evaluation.

IMPLICATION 5: BETTER INCLUSION OF WOMEN

Most of faith-based peacebuilding work focuses on clergy, which, traditionally, have been mostly men. Women are often marginalized in these processes, and consequently, their perspectives and experiences are excluded. Many women of faith are actively involved in peacebuilding in their communities. In fact, studies have shown that women are particularly effective agents of social change and conflict resolution (Hayward 2012; Marshal et al. 2011; cf. the case study of Pakistani women in Chapter 10).

One recent attempt to better include women at various levels in conflict resolution processes are the current negotiations with the Taliban in Afghanistan. Zalmay Khalilzad, Special Representative for Afghanistan Reconciliation at the US State Department, proposes a formula that not only includes senior government officials in the negotiations, but also representatives of the political opposition, of civil society, and in particular, women (Al Jazeera 2019). Khalilzad's approach represents the growing recognition that for too long the vital contributions of women in processes of conflict resolution and reconciliation have been sidelined.

IMPLICATION 6: BETTER INCLUSION OF THE YOUTH

At the same time, more attention in conflict resolution theory and praxis must be directed towards the youth. While the so-called "youth bulge" in many countries of the Global South has already given rise to concern about potential destabilizing effect, its tremendous potential goes largely neglected. Children and youths are often the most vulnerable group and those most severely affected by conflict. Engaging them in peacebuilding and trust building activities, for instance, through interreligious partnerships between local synagogues, churches, and mosques, is therefore critical. Youth leaders such as Malala Yousafzai and Greta Thunberg show the remarkable transformative power of young people that can quickly grow in outreach from a local to a national and even global scale.

Given the wide scope of SDG 16, SDG 4 (quality education and SDG 5 (gender equality) are of particular importance. The current UNHCR report on refugees and education shows that more than half of the children who had to leave their home, often due to violent conflict, have no opportunity to attend school. Yet children and youths who do not attend schools are more likely to be involved in child labor or criminal activity, gangs, and militias. Filuppo Grandi, UN High Commissioner for Refugees, points to the direct connection between peace and educating the youth by arguing "Education will prepare refugee children and youth for the world of today and of tomorrow. In turn, it will make that world more resilient, sustainable and peaceful" (UNHCR 2019: 9).

IMPLICATION 7: BETTER ENGAGEMENT OF THE MEDIA

Connected to the need to better include the youth is the need for conflict resolution in general, and religious conflict resolution in particular, to become better in strategically engaging the media and social media. The events connected with the so-called Arab Spring, for example, were largely driven by the youth and (social) media. And while there is no shortage of media outlets preaching religious hatred and intolerance—ISIS, for example, demonstrated how the media can be used creatively and effectively to disseminate their message of fear and destruction—religious peacebuilders have to catch up in employing these powerful instruments for the means of peace and tolerance.

Abu-Nimer points to three stumbling blocks on the way to successfully engaging the media (Abu-Nimer 2015). First, the existing religious media outlets are often part of the problem rather than the solution by promoting intolerance or even outright violence. This holds true for countries like Iraq, Afghanistan, or Somalia, as well as the Western communities such as ultra conservative evangelicals in the US. Second, especially in the Western hemisphere, many media outlets are influenced by the post-Enlightenment paradigm which regards religion as utterly private with no legitimate relevance for the public sphere. Accordingly, many media outlets lack religious literacy necessary to adequately understand and represent the religious dimension of many public issues. Third, religious peacemaking is usually not regarded as the most interesting type of news and therefore deemed neglectable. Filmmaker Wim Wenders points to the difficulties in portraying peace contrary to the more "exciting" violence (Wenders and Zournazi 2013).

IMPLICATION 8: TAKING THE ISSUES OF PROSELYTIZATION AND INSTRUMENTALIZATION INTO ACCOUNT

Religious actors often face the charge that their main goal is to attract followers and convert others. "The fear of conversion often comes up in interfaith engagement and it is not unfounded, because numerous traditions do contain a mandate to spread the faith" (Garred and Abu-Nimer 2018: 12). This can be a serious impediment to peacebuilding between religious groups. At the same time, one needs to acknowledge that conversion is not an exclusively religious phenomenon. Rather, "Both secular and faith-based organizations are engaged in some form of conversion. … All organizations aim to transform the way people in developing countries think and operate" (Heist and Cnaan 2016: 12). In the case study of post-genocide Rwanda, for instance, conversion and evangelization were named as explicit goals of the Christian churches in the context of reconciliation and development, without, however, making it a prerequisite for service delivery. This sensitive subject should therefore be treated in a differentiated manner and framed under the aspects of transparency and equality. If there is a goal of religious conversion, is it made transparent? Is service delivery independent of religious affiliation? Negative answers to these questions would indicate a problematic view on proselytization and the possible instrumentalization of service delivery for religious purposes.

IMPLICATION 9: BETTER ENGAGEMENT OF INDIGENOUS AND NON-ABRAHAMIC RELIGIONS

With much of Western attention focusing on the Abrahamic religions—Judaism, Christianity, and Islam—in conflict resolution, little attention is being paid to the contributions of indigenous and dharmic traditions (Hayward 2012: 6–7). Similar to Abrahamic faiths, these traditions have a wealth of resources and values that promote peacebuilding and justice, and many religious actors in these traditions play critical roles in their communities to resolve conflicts. Therefore, there is a pressing need for academics, policy makers, and practitioners to engage these traditions to broaden and deepen the field (Hayward 2012: 7).

Religions for Peace is an example of a multi-religious coalition that engages in common action for peace amongst the world's religious communities. As the world's largest and most representative multi-religious network engaged in promoting peace, Religions for Peace engages local communities from the grassroot level to senior political leaders. At the 10th World Assembly in Lindau, Germany, in 2019, Religions for Peace adopted the Peace Charter for Forgiveness and Reconciliation. Its preamble states,

> The vision of the Peace Charter for Forgiveness and Reconciliation is that the process of forgiving is vital if healing and reconciliation are to take place, as part of our collective efforts to seek justice, harmony and sustainable peace. Fostering and practicing forgiveness has the power to transform memories and deep-seated responses to legacies of injustice, conflict and war. … Faith and spiritual traditions guide and inspire us to awaken the best of our human potential, by practicing compassion, mercy, kindness, love, forgiveness and reconciliation, and to positively reshape our destinies.
>
> (Peace Charter for Forgiveness and Reconciliation 2019)

REFERENCES

Abu-Nimer, Mohammed. (2015). "Religion and Peacebuilding: Reflections on Current Challenges and Future Prospects", *Journal of Interreligious Studies*, 16: 14–29. Viewed from https://irstudies.org/journal/religion-and-peacebuilding-reflections-on-current-challenges-and-future-prospects-by-mohammed-abu-nimer-2/ [Date accessed October 30, 2019].

Abu-Nimer, Mohammed and Augsburger, David. (2009). *Peace-Building By, Between, and Beyond Muslims and Evangelical Christians.* Lanham, MD: Lexington Books.

Al Jazeera. (2019). "Intra-Afghan Negotiations to Follow US-Taliban Deal: Khalilzad", July 28, 2019. Viewed from www.aljazeera.com/news/2019/07/intra-afghan-negotiations-follow-taliban-deal-khalilzad-190728061121496.html [Date accessed October 30, 2019].

Garred, Michelle and Abu-Nimer, Mohammed (eds.). (2018). *Making Peace with Faith. The Challenges of Religion and Peacebuilding.* Lanham, MD: Rowman & Littlefield.

Hayward, Susan. (2012). "Religion and Peacebuilding. Reflections on Current Challenges and Future Prospects". United States Institute of Peace Special Report, Washington, DC. Viewed from www.usip.org/sites/default/files/SR313.pdf [Date accessed October 30, 2019].

Heist, Dan and Cnaan , Ram, A. (2016). "Faith-Based International Development Work: A Review", *Religion,* 7(19): 1–17.

Institute for Justice and Reconciliation (IJR). (2003). *South African Reconciliation Barometer.* Viewed from www.ijr.org [Date accessed October 30, 2019].

Marshall, Katherine, Hayward, Susan, Zambra, Claudia, Breger, Esther, and Jackson, Sarah. (2011). *Women in Religious Peacebuilding,* Washington, DC: United States Institute of Peace. Viewed from www.usip.org/publications/ 2011/05/women-religious-peacebuilding [Date accessed October 30, 2019].

McDonagh, Philip. (2018). *Religion and Security-Building in the OSCE Context.* Involving Religious Leaders and Congregations in Joint Efforts, ed. by OSCE Network. Viewed from http://osce-network.net/file-OSCE-Network/Publications/Religion_and_Security-Building_in_the_OSCE_Context_final.pdf [Date accessed October 30, 2019].

Pathfinders. (2017). *The Roadmap for Peaceful, Just and Inclusive Societies.* Viewed from https://cic.nyu.edu/sites/default/files/sdg16_roadmap_en_20sep17. pdf [Date accessed October 30, 2019].

Peace Charter for Forgiveness and Reconciliation. (2019). *Peace Charter for Forgiveness and Reconciliation.* Viewed from www.charterforforgiveness.org [Date accessed October 30, 2019].

Storrar, William F. and Andrew, R. Morton (eds.). (2004). *Public Theology for the 21st Century.* London: T&T Clark.

UN High Commissioner for Refugees (UNHCR). (2019). *Stepping up. Refugee Education in Crisis.* Viewed from https://unhcrsharedmedia.s3.amazonaws. com/2019/Education-report_30-August_2019/Education+Report+2019-Final-web.pdf [Date accessed October 30, 2019].

Vader, Jennie. (2015). "Meta-Review of Inter-Religious Peacebuilding Program Evaluations". CDA Collaborative Learning Projects as part of the Peacebuilding Evaluation Consortium. Viewed from https:// allianceforpeacebuilding.org/wp-content/uploads/2018/06/PEC_ MetaEvaluation-of-IRPB-Program-Evaluations.pdf [Date accessed October 30, 2019].

Wenders, Wim and Zournazi, Mary. (2013). *Inventing Peace. A Dialogue on Perception.* New York: Palgrave Macmillan.

INDEX

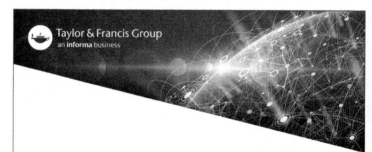

Printed in the United States
by Baker & Taylor Publisher Services